Psalms for the Poor

Psalms for the Poor

Kent Gramm

RESOURCE *Publications* • Eugene, Oregon

PSALMS FOR THE POOR

Copyright © 2015 Kent Gramm. All rights reserved. Except for brief quotations in critical publications or reviews, no part of this book may be reproduced in any manner without prior written permission from the publisher. Write: Permissions. Wipf and Stock Publishers, 199 W. 8th Ave., Suite 3, Eugene, OR 97401.

Resource Publications
An Imprint of Wipf and Stock Publishers
199 W. 8th Ave., Suite 3
Eugene, OR 97401

www.wipfandstock.com

ISBN 13: 978-1-4982-2597-7

Manufactured in the U.S.A.   07/09/2015

for Robert

Psalm 1

the law of the Lord

1

This is the Law. The Law is everything:
a sad man cherishing a slice of pumpkin
pie, a wife of dreamy cream beside him
snowy white and fluffed, the winter sun dim
through the coffee shop window, many voices
moaning round of romance. This is a race
of rock-loving farmers and brooding, pacing
kings, cancer in the genes. There are no choices.
Glaciers melt in Odysseus's face;
Athena looks around and packs it in,
reports to God that everything done brings
unintended consequences. "There's grace,"
God says with a sly everlasting grin.
The memory of love checks her watch, sings.

2

But I was saying, everything is Law—
the brooks, stones, companionship, suffering.
How does a constellation wheel? Its spring
is in the numbers dribbling along awe
like jewelly bread crumbs. It's all in numbers,
all of it, right down to the ants. And chance
is covered too, explainable to parents
on a planet circling Arcturus—blurs
in our best telescopes but intelligent.
Nothing is, that is not the Law. Always
two plus two is four; passion is always
red, purity blue, Son of God argent;
I will always remember you. I sit
with the sun going down, and this is it.

3

Can it be written in a book, the Law?
Some book, with pages like accordions,
print vigorous as spermatozoa,
punctuation bright as a million suns,
an index hot and right as algebra—
its states like H_2O a trinity
transforming on the page, liquid fiction
crystallizing with a sheen: history
now, nonfiction, suffering and death—"one
damn thing after another"—how it bleeds
its ink! And then, the last chapter a gas,
white-winged horses farther than eye can see
converge to Brahman minuscule and vast,
a Way that rises into poetry.

*He shall be like a tree planted by the rivers of water,
that bringeth forth his fruit in his season.*

Unless I touch his hand and lay my fingers
to his healing side I'll say he's a ghost,
like King Saul or Auntie Maud—in the clothes
of my low brain, that will see anything
I want to see. But my hand is something
else—it won't lie to me, it won't believe;
it was this that plucked the fruit off the tree
in the Garden and it knows everything

and nothing. You will call me The Doubter.
I will believe only what I can feel
and nothing I am told. Words are nothing,
but when I feel His hand like living water
I will draw it to me like a willow tree
and I will believe; so all in its season.

Psalm 2 (a)

Why do the heathen rage?

The heathen rage because they hate our freedoms,
and their brides desire our televisions sets.
They crave attention and our Happy Meals;
they wish they could play for the New York Jets;
they wish they could be all that they can be.
The more we give, the more they try to get.
They are crazy to be Americans.
Give them half a chance and they'd be Cheyennes,
Santee Sioux, Mescalero Apaches,
the Last Mohicans, Crees, Arapahos,
or what have you—you know the litany—
so they could get handouts and casinos.
They've seen that baby playing on the dirt
floor in Mississippi, and they want her.

Psalm 2 (b)

Why do the Christians rage? the heathen ask.
Why do they trumpet prayer like sounding brass?
Why do they shove their muzzles up our ass?
The Christians rage because they hate their freedoms
and everyone else's—but then again,
since when do Christians rage? These believers
are something else: they have taken the name
in vain—squandered the term on righteousness,
kidnapped Jesus, and left us sinners stunned
at Calvary. The god they worship hates
pale light through summer blinds, reflected sun
on morning walls, its shadow-barred white
beside the Mediterranean bed,
the glass of last night's wine, the sacred head.

Psalm 3

Lord, how are they increased that trouble me!

We don't believe in demons any more,
but disbelief was never a deterrent
to invisibles. Specters are stronger
than I am. Modesty forbids mention
of whom and what I have antagonized
by mere existence, but a wet dragon
the size of Manhattan licks my brain
in his sleep. The Lord does not let him wake.

A tapeworm wants me and I can't prevent him.
He came wrapped in glass – Satan sent him.
He is real, but God will not invent him.

I sow and knead and shape my waking bread:
the consequences drink my dreams like blood.
I will lie with the dead. I will see God.

Psalm 4 (a)

Stand in awe, and sin not

What? Sin not? Good luck with that. Just to stand
these days is sin; in fact, could there be greater
sin than doing nothing?—than pretending
innocence when Wall Street knocks at the door
and homeless children blow up like balloons,
full of Co2, tuberculosis,
other people's prosperity, and doom.
See them floating above the skyscrapers
wise as serpents and innocent as doves,
red, yellow, blue; interesting as newspapers,
"all breathing human passion far above,"
giving this old world everything they've got.
See them passing. Stand in awe and sin not.

Psalm 4 (b)

Stand in awe, and sin not: commune
with your own heart upon your bed

Pure awe is incompatible with sin.
Just try to sin when you have put your nicest
Aurora Borealis on, Orion's
favorite, and wait for him to notice.
Ah, what can we do but our best? Work well,
try to be sane and healthy, try to love.
And when the daily infinite feels stale,
when you have nothing worth saving to save,
then commune with your heart upon your bed.
Consider the heart. It is everything.
Once Orion was a man, it is said,
like any other man. He heard you sing,
was the lucky difference. He stood in awe
until his heart became a field of stars.

Psalm 5

Lead me, O Lord, in thy righteousness

But what it is, God's righteousness, who knows?
The brain is broccoli, and muscles peel
like cabbage shards, the joints are garlic cloves
in red threads: the body is a cow.

Where does God's righteousness even begin?
In the brain? In the rules? In how we feel?
All these separate here there and then now.
The mind is a cracked glass: we are insane.

God's righteousness is wholeness, everything
here and now; only what is whole is real.
It would be righteous to know this, but how?
Faith says so. Everything but faith is sin.

Devils look up and love us the wrong way—
piece by piece: sex, viscera, tongue, eyes, brain.
But God alone is lover of the soul,
always everywhere suffering and whole.

Psalm 6 (a)

O Lord, rebuke me not in thine anger

These bones are nothing—human bones are leaves
in waxed paper—but I am stuck in them;
I am my veins, my thoughts are smeared on them:
where does love begin and my corpus end?
You are the beginning of the end. You
are what I am not and are what I am
and on the page you say you are I AM.
My heart is paper, a veined pressed leaf

that lies on the sea of salt where it fell.
For I have sinned and am a fool, alone
in an old ocean, lost, at home on bones,
becoming comfortable with myself:
as far as anyone knows, good in bed—
the satin one, where you stay when you're dead.

Psalm 6 (b)

Depart from me, all ye workers of iniquity.

What shall we do to work the works of God?
"Believe." Iniquity works by itself.
Would you be pure, be pure belief in God
and in whom He has sent. None of this help
for the other side, the mills and engines
of iniquity. Work in the pure Word.
On bad days I am friction—grit and grime—
in the motor of the Ford of the Lord;
on good days I'm a Fifty-Seven Chevy,
small block two-barrel, two hundred fifty
cubes of honey-smooth exuberance: me,
a classic two-tone, steering-mounted shifter.
Juice me up with ethyl, I become all creed;
avenues of asphodel dissolve in speed.

Psalm 7 (a)

God is angry with the wicked every day.

The wrath of blood. Expose it to the air,
and blood wants blood—like water wants the sea,
like fire wants dry company:
everything compensates the nothing that things were.
It must be seen to be appreciated,
the wrath of God. Expose it to the air
and we inhale the icy glass of terror,
reasonably. Lenience is over-rated
in matters of moral accuracy.
No sin goes to waste. We shovel our own
bladders and livers onto our own plates
and knock up hot mock-ups of our own facts.
Dust to dust, seed to seed—it all returns
under the sun and at full speed, daily:
glaciers steaming, bleeding into the sea.

Psalm 7 (b)
return thou on high

The Lord on high is just and fair,
and righteous to a fault;
He is a god when he's up there,
presiding over all.

Down here he/she's another thing—
invisible as salt
in use, more intimate than sin;
if found, then found at fault.

A lord almighty's dignity
requires the proper place—
a mausoleum in the sky,
not someone's beat-up face.

A deity conceived is free
to be, to will, to do—
not troubled by contingency,
not breathing next to you.

Psalm 8

When I consider thy heavens . . .

Thy heavens frighten me, to tell the truth.
This little Earth's speed is a constant shock;
you'd think our air would fall off like a sack.
And then where do you go to take a breath?—
the next atmosphere is light years away
and it's a soup of half-frozen methane.

But then I think that speed is relative,
and distance too. My thought masters it all.
I am the lord of all that I survey:
you reduce everything that you believe.
There's no catch. I'm as simple as the rain,
and all I have to do is fall.

Psalm 9 (a)
the Lord shall endure forever

Eternity could not exist except
in God; tomorrow is nothing unless
its soul is God; and today is a vast
Korsakov's Syndrome, blank, total, and rapt.
Then let us ride the emptiness like fleas
on a blind pachyderm—not only blind
but lobotomized; not merely mindless
but possessed of the blitzed sensibilities
of true believers who have been drinking
paint—proud of its size because it is blind,
philosophically indifferent to fleas,
without moral responsibilities
if God is a wad of liberal thinking
in a transient Jewish carpenter's mind.

Psalm 9 (b)
the Lord shall endure forever

Could God die?—but there is no subjunctive
for God and death except for Nazareth.
Take that moment, then: Pontius Pilate lives
but all meaning has exhaled its last breath.
Now what? Pretend nothing happens reversing
the disappointment—no resurrection
and no Amazing Grace: sheer mere perversion
of everything worth claiming, perfection
of imperfectability. Now we
climb our minds like cats; we grow long white beards;
we shoulder the writhing wild cross of Why;
we say, To hell with it all, one more beer
for the Empire. What a nightmare, what a danger,
what a goblin gurgling in a manger.

Psalm 9 (c)

let not man prevail . . . that the nations may know themselves to be but men.

If You hear all things, then what do You hear:
stretched stiff in rags in graves, their prayers all said,
are their old words living words, the lost poor,
the liquidated, eradicated
mothers, fathers, children burned up in wars;
are they still preying on Your sacred head
alive? When one child loses attention
and is left there, is raped or given a gun
or preached to, coughing, in a long alley—
do You finally have a heart and listen, then?
Will You do something—terrible—finally?—
so nations know themselves to be but men?

Ps. 9 (d)

The needy shall not always be forgotten:
the expectation of the poor shall not perish for ever.

CALIN

1

A quiet, gentle boy, he always was,
and small; the dark eyes of a dying deer.
"What would you do with a million dollars?"
we asked him when he was ten—some fifteen years
ago. He smiled. "I would buy potatoes!"
He lifted up a board and pointed down:
there was a two-foot space under the floor.
"I would fill it with potatoes—good, brown
potatoes." "But a million would buy more,"
we said. "What else would you buy?" "I would buy
bananas."
    They held his funeral outdoors
because no church knew them. A public shrine
would have to do for him, the gathered poor
his passing bells, his drawing-down of blinds.

2

There are no answers for the poor.
The world will not call itself to account,
or stand up to answer an outraged Lord.
The poor will simply have to do without,
because there is no sentiment out here.
And though we know irony feeds no one,
its wry illusions medicate our fears.
A very poor man has lost a good son.
A mother, sister, brother are alone
somewhere in the rags of early March snow.
They will have to do without him today.
Tired charcoal-faced miners will come and go;
priests down in the village will always pray
to Father, Son, inconsolable Ghost;
family pays. There is no other way.

3

The rich may die a thousand ways, a poor
boy only one. A stark simplicity
led him to the clinic's fathomless door
for the inoculation: it was free.
The dirty needle gave him HIV
so quietly; lungs shrunken with TB
cost too much to fix: he exhaled his blood.
No mystery: he died of poverty.

If we are evil, can the Lord be good?
The Lord has taken, and the Lord has taken;
but we have done the dirty work ourselves.
There might be other worlds less God-forsaken;
we have our own heaven and our own hell
right here meanwhile, and these coal-gutted hills
will echo his voice, if anything will.

4

His father says he'll leave the hospital
and come back home. His mind has broken down.
He saw everything; he was there at the end;
he heard the verdict from the busy doctor;
stood with cold wind blowing his ghostly hair
at the little funeral. Oh, he will
come back, and the light in his wonderful
eyes will make us so happy that the stars
will follow us to bed. We will be here
at this table, and he'll come up the path
and open the door, our Calin, happy
again, healthy, with color in his face,
so glad to see us and as good as new.
He believes this. And I believe it, too.

Psalm 10 (a)

thou hast heard the desire of the humble

When once You hear, it shall be done; You hear
before the mother of the supplicant
was born: we wait, but You who live and reign
eternally and in eternity
have done it long ago; You do it now
and always will: it is always not done
and always done—and that is what we are.

Why standest thou afar off, Lord?—never
seeing what we need, caring what we want,
leaving pledges and threats to come again
although the first visit to Galilee
was footsteps in water, breezes blowing
cinnamon sighs on the Rose of Sharon,
Ghost shrouded in the belly like a star.

Psalm 10 (b)

He lieth in wait secretly as a lion in his den: he lieth in wait to catch the poor: he doth catch the poor . . . Arise, O Lord; O God, lift up thine hand: forget not the humble.

What use are prayers? What use is anything?
The end, the purpose of it all—is what?
To glorify the Lord and enjoy him
forever. What use can be made of that?

The word *use*—"function," "service," benefit,"
"purpose" arrogates to us divinity.
Let God ask, "What's the use?"

                                He lies in wait;
he does catch the poor: what will be, will be.

She watches from her window, the woman on the hill:
the boys down at the river, swimming nude—
her hands float to her bosom, her heart does as it wills:
she's sixty and she's naked and they're lewd.
What is the use of anything? The poor
are dying in their heartbeats at the door.

Psalm 10 (c)

thou wilt prepare their heart

She lifts her hands to falling breasts.—Oh, heart,
wilt thou require my soul?—Oh, old desire
so faithful to its horror—praying fire,
vessel of incense that never burns out!
Her shadow rides a sacred horse: its wings
beat and thunder before her charcoal legs;
her veinless knees and thighs dissolve and dig,
pressing against those big silk ribs; fingers
clutch in that plunging mane. Then awakened,
panting, in the beauty of the lilies,
satin walls and pillow, terrified and raked
by grief strident as the last trumpet, cries
out to the Father Everlasting, who sees
her seed of abandon with the rain's eyes.

Psalm 11

In the Lord put I my trust: how say ye to my soul,
Flee as a bird to your mountain?

There is no refuge here outside the Lord,
but keep in mind that God does not protect
the doomed sweet-hearted whom we call elect.
Precious in His sight's the blood that's poured
from the poor. Blessed the uneducated
eating carbohydrates, can't afford
transportation to Trader Joe's, ignored,
drunk on other lives, sick and desperate.

The others can escape; they have jewelry.
They drive safe, well-engineered cars. Christians.
Jesus has tuberculosis: he dies
in his fat young mother's arms while she waits
in the Wal-Mart parking lot for her ride.
She has bought hair gel, and candy for him.

Psalm 12 (a)

*The words of the Lord are pure words, as silver
tried in a furnace of earth, purified seven times.*

Your words are pure, as silver tried
as silver purified
as worship in the eyes is pure
as worship in the eyes

reflects the soul of holiness
reflects the ghost of peace and rest—
love in silver, glass, a mirror
clear breast, all confessed.

Your word is tried
come down divine
in suffering and silver
in silver purified.

Psalm 12 (b)

*The wicked walk on every side,
when the vilest are exalted.*

1

He walks in wickedness like oil. His eyes
are large as syphilis in a Petri
dish, two cauliflowers looking at me,
two bunches. He is a huge, dripping fly.
He is all comprehension. He knows what
I want. He knows what everybody wants:
to enjoy ourselves like whores, to be bought
with gold we can bite, to wake up in luck.

Bad men, wicked men, have his confidence
and instincts: they penetrate your confusion
with a meaty handshake that makes you wince.
You have many gods and they have only one.
Their politics are commercial, their morals entertain;
they wait in their Mercedes in the cool afternoon rain.

2

When psalmists talk wickedness they mean me.
I have Roman tastes but I'm a bad bet
for pope. I take whatever I can get.
(Within limits, women like honesty.)
If the devil's in the details, I am
meticulous. I'm just saying. Jesus
was all heart, you know what I mean? He was
all heart: no thought, nothing, less than I AM.
The point being that I could use some heart.
Remember Jesus came not for the righteous
but for the sinners. The slinky witches
with caramel cars are running out of parts.
It won't be long before I'll need a ride,
a good road, bridge, someone on the other side.

Psalm 13

How long wilt thou forget me, O Lord? for ever?

Our woman hides her face; she hides her face
behind her hands; it is a plain and unmade
face, undignified as earth and as plain.
She smears the tears away and hides her face
and blubbers of her murdered son: *We won't
see him no more.* Her floral house dress sags
like sweaty bags. Her flat brownish hair prays
like rain; she is under water. The Lord
holds lights and camera and she cries into
them. The TV audience can't see her
eyes, just her man's chin and wrong nose. Do you
think her eyes might be beautiful if she
weren't alone? Her emptied son can't see her.
Poor, poor Rachael; it does no good to weep.

I will sing unto the Lord.

Rachael, will you love again? Will you sing
unto the Lord, a handmaid with your basket
running over with blue and white forget-me-nots,
in their star hearts God's forgotten gold ring?
In the waters of forgetfulness along
the Temple wall, do you wade the shadows
of the morning, your finger tracing sorrow
in blue, a silent melancholy song?
Or do you sit in your dim house all day
staring out a window at apartments,
TV?—your husband sitting unshaven
in a tee shirt with a can of cheap beer,
blue as Krishna, Jesus down from heaven,
not knowing what to do, half drunk but there.

Psalm 14 (a)

The fool hath said in his heart

1

If everything you have belongs to God,
and God is the reward of those who die
in faith, then what is bad and what is good?
What are the uses of adversity?

The answers of belief answer nothing.
The dinosaurs are in the rain; the air
is all there is to breathe. Your dirty wings
are all you've got to get from here to there.

The ink had hardly dried around the sun
when God Himself became a word, and then
all hell broke loose. Love is a smoking gun
if everything's to come around again.

Surrender. Give. It's a mirror—the glass
is your brain. This is all there is.

2

And then there is a face that is not yours,
more beautiful than anything you know.
You have your answer. "Look! It is the Lord."
Here, sit down. You look like you've seen a ghost.

And then He speaks, or She speaks. This is no
ghost or anything else that ever was—
pure being, always is: the spring wind blows
and never was not wind, and never *was*—

and you can't explain it because you're not
listening. The cool maenads fall to sleep
like sparks from fireworks, like water, like heat—
and the slice between past and future heals

like snow. Press the hand behind love, quiet
as a first light that hasn't spoken yet.

Psalm 14 (b)
They are all become filthy

1

Right here: this is where we see the Bible.
It's not God's mouthpiece, every jot and tittle.
God saying this—like a lousy sport, ginned
as hell, surprised, disgusted, complaining?
What God sees when looking down, looking in—
"looking" at all?—is beyond explaining
to the likes of us. To ascribe to Him
or Her a bald generalization
or worse, a theological thesis,
mixes blasphemy with absurdity.
No, the clean authority of Jesus
is not in this raging cursive poetry.

The poet, stung by someone trusted's treason,
suffers singing, praying his unreason.

2

He doesn't think to accuse God of treason,
doesn't clutch stubborn hands and sob his "Why?"
Everything happens for a reason
and God allows human perfidy,
inexplicably. Abused blame themselves,
though if God wants Canaanite blood, might he
not come home one night thirsty, or worse, filled
with that thickly animalian swill?
Horrible surprise? A spider the size
of a face in a mirror, a stomach head,
has sticky fingers sensitive as eyes
and curved teeth growing like nails on the dead,
has a mouth that dreams your softness; your skin
is its web. It bites, it bites; it hates sin.

Psalm 14 (c)
there is none that doeth good

This one is mighty hard to buy. We all
know people who do good—the soldier throwing
himself on a grenade, strong as he falls;
the mother washing floors for her son, knowing
he will graduate to firms in New York:
all sacrifice, all giving up the ghost
of evidence for the deep seed of love.
Still, St. Paul would not have anyone boast,
so he likes this verse, uses it to prove
that everything is grace, nothing our work.
But the psalm-singer was fed up with us,
been cheated on or sued, been to New York
with buckles on his shoes, spent all his trust.
We passed his wagon: "Oregon Or Bust."

You saw the bones of his oxen bleaching
and a Sioux arrow through his yarmulke.
Some warriors must have tired of his preaching
and said "Enough kvetch already. This schmuck
would ask the Great Spirit, 'So where's the beef?'
if partridges were showered from heaven,
if the rocks gave honey. Let us put heap
many arrows in his butt." No leaven
of humor mitigated the psalmist's
bitterness, or he would have crossed out *Or*
on his Conestoga's canvas before
stalking off—shafts in his ass and his fist
shaking "Why?"—across the purple prairie,
aware of whip-poor-wills, but not very.

In one way you can't blame him. His big dream—
an American dream, current since Moses
turned aside to see the bush in cold flame
and heard the call to let the people go—
that dream sizzled away under the glare
of the high sun's aboriginal stare.
When you believed in a moral failure
you're disillusioned with humanity;
you sip your religion without ice, pure;
and you make demands that others can't meet.
You say, I quit; to hell with Oregon.
You let the Indians and Army fight.
You dream wagons crazy in the heavens,
rocking in the ruts of Elder Night.

Psalm 15 (a)

Lord, who shall abide in thy tabernacle . . . ?
He that . . . speaketh the truth in his heart.

Gentlemen pay, but she's a virgin rose,
young tongue curved like a petal, smooth and soft
like silk on a lion's thigh, poured awful
with sex in a Bangkok bar. She says "Oh—"
as if her last glass tiger were dying
of explosions in its groin—very good
for a teen-aged wraith made of sandalwood
fragrance. Of course he knows she is lying
and he likes it that way. His lie is white
and as old as Cain. She sinks to her knees
bleeding her diamonds like the Pleiades,
so rich that she is unable to rise,
beseeching the sea of its deepest prayer.
She can't see his scar but she knows it's there.

Psalm 15 (b)

Lord, who shall abide in thy tabernacle . . . ?
He that . . . speaketh the truth in his heart.

Can one heart's truth be Lincoln and My Lai?—
our love for justice, selfless and enduring;
and our lost millions of forgotten poor
with simple dreams (food, heat, shelter), who die
scraping the papers of our principles.
Our truth is two truths of shame and honor,
Luther's *simul iustus et peccator*—
almost chosen sinners. Was it simpler
fifty years ago, that summer Bobby
Kennedy went down to Mississippi
and held a poor child in his arms, tears in his eyes,
asking, "How can this country allow it?" Good night,
all princes. You want Americans to be kind;
you want one truth, a purer dream, a braver lie.

Psalm 15 (c)

*He that sweareth to his own hurt,
and changeth not.*

Scent of peonies, shower of honey-
suckle—a fragrance desperate for breath,
the full ripe agony of dying May,
stamen waving outrageous raging red,
a showgirl's legs in every memory
and angels wearing sequins and silk tulle,
lips like a soul: but I swear you away.
Were you pale, were you beautiful and nude
as Michelangelo's hypotheses,
I wouldn't touch you, only look at you,
holding to my web of Eumenides,
dead sober, my clean skin glued to the view,
ecstatically cool about the great void,
obedient to the commands of God.

Psalm 16

thou wilt not leave my soul in hell . . .
in thy presence is fulness of joy

Have I myself? I stir the fur of sable
against my bare ovaries; my dear breasts
are whole globes like mercury; the frail
aura within my slender pale I grasp
like a young olive tree. With tender feet
I wade in a Magellanic Cloud up
to my articulated lips, breathe,
and the universe comes in, dust to dust—

and see God, a vision. Have I nothing?
I am a maiden's dream, a maiden sleeping
in the arms of her dream, a dream breathing,
gold in a snow of gold, light in light. To be.
You are the beginning. Before nothing
was, you kissed me, you slept sweetly with me.

Psalm 17 (a)

thou hast visited me in the night

I wake at night in a shivering chill.
Ice races in my veins and I can't stop
shaking; reach for light but a ghastly thrill
on my bared arm shocks like a pistol shot.
So cold. What have I got? What have I got?
Only God. Only God. Holding a bill,
the undertaker stands there on the porch—
you can smell the chemicals—dressed for work
but the Lord quietly crosses the bed
and tells him No, He tells him Not quite yet,
comes back wipes the devil's mark off the mirror
but does not say everything is O. K.,
says without having to say, I am here,
and I say, Stay, whatever happens, stay.

Psalm 17 (b)

*Keep me as the apple of the eye, hide me
under the shadow of thy wings*

O keep me as the apple of your eye,
hide me under the shadow of your wings,
for I have sunk myself in desperate dreams;
I act as though I'm never going to die.
Last night a woman called me in my sleep.
She wore no wings and was not beautiful
but I belonged to her, happy jack and all.
I woke up optimistic but it didn't keep.
It rotted with consciousness, or waking.
Cicadas are up this year in billions:
holes in the ground, a creepy awaking
all at once after seventeen years, tons
of dead bugs, big red eyes, translucent wings,
dry streets drifted with paper skeletons.

Psalm 17 (c)

I shall be satisfied, when I awake,
with thy likeness.

The verse has no inside and no outside.
I write this when asleep and dream of being
awake; I will see only what God seems,
and yet the dreamed waked self is satisfied.
What is the waking and what is the dream?
Surely the text's "awake" must mean I've died,
but "likeness" as illusion must need eyes.
It seems what is, is seen as what it seems.

I think the likeness is all we can get,
all that is. Behind this dream is one dreaming.
Dream know dreamer? All we dream is the dream.
But to know the likeness as Yours: just that
is the turning inside-out of the Earth,
the burst into the dreamer's arms of birth.

Psalm 18

I will love thee, O Lord

1

I spent the summer teaching her to dance,
a tough old girl with muscles in her pants.
The bars up north were dark and wet and loud
and she was anything but proud;
she knew I wanted her and knew what for,
but had a trap where some girls have a door.
Still, I was good at gnawing off a leg
and what I couldn't jimmy I could beg.
So then the cow goes pregnant, says it's me,
and here we are. Let's see what we can see:
I could go back up there and settle down
with thirteen kids, a whore, a thorny crown—
or stay and keep my peas down in the pod.
The ones that need you fill your shoes with lead.
I cut her down like butter, dreamed I was dead,
and woke up like this, just hollow for God.

2

To love the Lord is youth: I will be young
again in love of you. I will not know
what I know now. My memory is strong
but soluble, and somewhere long ago
it could have wandered into a different place
along the river, and I would not be
the selfish, corrupt mess you have today.
I would suffer in your arms constantly,
wanting to be out of this skin and in
you, purely wanting not to be any
me at all except knowing to be in
you, being and not-being, one, many:
pure again, mountains, morning, sunrise, dew—
in love again with only, only you.

3

Lord, I would love you as the rivers do—
in their courses, but take me at the flood;
I want to do whatever angels do
but do it hot, with summer in my blood.
I want to love you through a holy raven
of a woman, through her like a river
down the slippery banks of night, taken
by the salty delta, taken right.
I wear a flat-brimmed hat of creamy felt,
a suit of white gardenias slick as silk,
a ruffled shirt as tissuey as milk—
a lady's hands for suspenders and belt:
but I can take it all off, gamble hard
and risk my panting mouth on your wet star.

4

I'd love you as the everlasting dark,
the hole of my soul, with nothing but you;
or if I must, love you as a steep hawk
loves the laws of physics—with its nature:
pure, unabated by prayer, terrible
with sight. But if all I could ever have
were the flat, soft, humanly possible,
then I beg and I pray please make me rave
with tender, loving faith—anything but
this theological, thin-lipped wonder
I've been taught—mad, a naked lunatic
thinking the moon is you, embracing where
there is nothing, my brain turning a trick,
but waking to the light I swore was there.

Psalm 19 (a)
The heavens declare the glory of God

Space. Pure physics, mathematics, nothing
moral here—no killing sheep, no bleating
tongues and wild eyes wondering and reading
the religious heart; galaxies going
nowhere until they burn out like old faiths,
hard stones of dead stars as dark as prayer,
purple ionic clouds spectacular,
all dust and fire and all passing away.
Terror. What a mind to perish into
as a fetus slips into her decay—
earth, the heaven of imagination
waiting like a formula—a God who
can brave his own mind, can love creation.

Psalm 19 (b)

Who can understand his errors?

I did the only decent thing: I sent
her off with him in the last boat. They saw
me small and smaller on this island, a law
to myself and alone. Wave. Goodbye, Kent.
I write this knowing no one will read it
but God. I live for myself and for God—
I think; maybe only for myself. God
might be in my imagination. This
would then never be read at all. No one
else is here, ever will be. I will die
here. I will build a church, for I am done
with loving anyone else. It is my
church, and I will sit in its door and stare
to sea until my eyes are white with prayer.

Psalm 20 (a)

*The Lord . . . grant thee according to
thine own heart*

Bury me in dreams, enrose me in hope,
and lower me through the soil of despair.
Leave me to God. I am a soul enclosed
in the happenstance of what I desire,
a heart made of God cored in who I am,
forgetfulness awash in baptism:
bury me in dreams. Send me a woman,
a pony of fire, a blessing of sin,
a child; send blood from the Fountain of Youth
in cascading sacraments until I am
too drunk to dream of anything but truth;
engold me in the sun-sown snow of OM.
You, the only awake, Lord, bury me
in your dreams. Whatever is, let it be.

Psalm 20 (b)

Now know I that the Lord saveth
his anointed

You have to learn it for yourself; no-one
can tell you: the seed of life is not-knowing,
a dark rose in the core of the soul's stone;
it is the Lord. A monk in a gold robe's
folds sits in his soul in perpetual sun
and bows each day in emptiness, praying
for night. The grown gold and odorous gums
of Eden—lost! in the grasp of Satan's
knowing. The God who answers prayer is true,
a servant of the Lord and sovereign over
His illusion; but the Old One is new:
no knowing and no answer and no power.
The One Soul knows, unknowing; knows, being—
is unknown, is All, is the blind eye seeing.

Psalm 21

so will we sing and praise thy power

1

What if there is no Will of God?—power
being nothing more than human nightmare.
Your average mouse is an image of terror—
all eyes in the claws of a horned owl,
all finality, disillusionment,
and pain telescoped into its round mouth—
a scale model of hard biblical truth.
The owl converges to a furry point
like the Big Bang in reverse. What a will!
Power to burn. Pointless if you don't need
to eat, but it's sure impressive as hell.
Jesus as mouse is the world's worst metaphor—
the Son of God shrinking, coming here to bleed,
and everything else rising up to kill.

2

Instead of Will let's talk about Presence.
There is nothing else. Flies have it. We should
have it too—not "it" but the Present Tense.
The lake's surface tonight will turn to gold,
then later, trailing across it like pollen,
the depthless history of the Ghost Road—
all light still flying from when it began:
God the way, the truth, and the life, unknown
suddenly here, and every second more so
and more, and more, world without end Amen
for when it ends it shall begin again
like a metaphor for a metaphor
within which "Will" is a shrunk, bleeding word,
livid history of the Living Lord.

3

The housefly has a thousand eyes, enough
to see me coming—judge, jury,
clumsy executioner, for whom germs
claim the attention like a thousand gods.
That's a lot of eyes and a lot of gods.

The Real Presence must be a sacrament—
a widow finding a lost coin, a pearl
worth everything, an old and warming world.
You call it your last will and testament.
Leave it, and move on to some other world

where creatures can be made to see better,
the Holy Ghost isn't a metaphor
but word, will, being, together itself
and moves on the water, gold with power.

Psalm 22 (a)

My God, my God, why hast thou forsaken me?

Life is difficult. Then you die.
If you have no idea why,
it is difficult to repent.
If you have done no wrong, more why.

You know nothing until too late.
The baby cicadas crawl out
of their holes, drop their clothing,
and bumble around copulating

by the bushel, meanwhile droning
that chattering racket, homing
in on each other to get laid,
armor on armor. It's holy,

at least innocent—no one's paid—
and they've been created that way.
So my question is, Why the hell
does their creator walk away?

In a month they're dead as their shells,
corpses everywhere, and the smell
is ravaging. The difference
between them and us I can't tell.

Presumably the Lord's defense
is that they don't have the Bible,
guilt, souls, intentions, consequences.
But I have heard them groan like lambs.
On their backs, their legs spell like hands.
They do suffer. And they repent.

Psalm 22 (b)

Last night the sky was awful—spent
like nickels. Wonder where it went.
It's bad for man to be alone.
We think we are the firmament.

We got it back this morning, though,
but worse for wear: it's full of smoke
or something, worse than yesterday.
Time's running out; let's go for broke

and find each other. Get our fill
before the Chinese eat our hills
and Arabs buy all our water.
We could kiss each other, pay bills,

have colds, at night sleep together
aging through to God together
and you would keep alive my soul.
That's love, isn't it? Unsevered?

Psalm 23 (a)

The Lord is my shepherd

The Lord is the shepherd, the Lord is the lamb,
the Lord is the dawn that swallows the sun:
Creator, Preserver, Dissolver—the One
worshipped in myriads, manifest, unknown—
the Way that is nameless, the holy I AM,
Krishna and Jesus, the dark of the soul,
the Buddha who smiles and the Buddha who knows.
You are the legend who walks on still waters,
the Word and the deed brooding on water—
the snow of the Ghost Road sparkling on water—
green pasture, warm meadow, shadow of home,
lotus of the soul: descend like a dove.
Come golden rose and New Jerusalem,
come Spirit of Wisdom, Spirit of Love.

Psalm 23 (b)

I shall not want.

I shall be dead. "How are you?" Can't complain.
"Is there anything you need?" Not a thing.
Streets in Paris will shine wet in the spring
but I won't need aspirin for the pain.
The sweet rue will put forth her tender shoots
but my attention will be focused stone.
All the girls I never met who live alone
can dress in lace and patent leather boots
for all I'll care—I am finally on the path
of righteousness, mixing with still water,
at last one and the same with a green pasture.
Eat your heart out, world; there's no more love here.
Then, in an endless dream of home, alone
with everything, alone with God's warm soul—

Psalm 23 (c)

He restoreth my soul

In Hebron and Damascus and Baghdad
some questions have been raised. At the North Pole
a gaggle of dispossessed Eskimos
muse like Lutherans about what they had
before things changed. In Chicago it's bad—
lots to clean up and July unbearable—
but Bangladesh is worse: people huddle
inland like Trojans losing the *Iliad*.
Fortunately, we will all live again.
They've discovered lately that the City
of God is planned out like a wheel within
a wheel, as in Ezekiel's vision,
or like a flattened eyeball that can see
all around its two skin-thin dimensions.

Psalm 23 (d)

he restoreth my soul

He brings me back to life—not born again
but doing something after I can't do
it any more, the child I used to be
remembered in the skill of nerves and bones
like side-arming a baseball in a dream and the dream true:
a small synecdoche
for how it works—how it all works, time
and eternity, space and character—
the stage an image of the actor,
the poem an understudy of the rhyme.
Now my soul is made, the second time
around, the face learning from its mirror
a possibility of error;
the poem spelled out from a completed rhyme.

Psalm 24

the Lord mighty in battle

I want to know if Jesus is the Lord
of Hosts, is terrible on battlefields,
presides like a scythe where my daughter bleeds,
weakens enemies' knees by his clean word—
he who blessed the unarmed suffering meek,
raised up a little girl by his hand's touch,
fed multitudes within his voice's reach,
and died dead for sinners like you and me.
Or do the holy Persons disagree?—
the Father high on righteous power of course;
the Spirit motherly, and no divorce;
the Son a victim of the Trinity
as we conceive of them, it, him, or her:
the heart's armies, and the heart is at war.

Psalm 25
the Way

"The Way" implies a place to go, an end—
a heaven, let us say; but then there's death,
possessing all we know. Reach the goal, then
what? "Welcome home; you are under arrest."
The Way might be the only road there is,
alpha to omega; the circle bends
like space around a very heavy sun,
love the ragged fabric of this dimension.
Might be, it is a Person. You are All
there is: You who are the Way are the Life,
the candle-lit cranberry birth canal,
the mourner marrying husband and wife;
over the hill, the only whip-poor-will
singing where the wind and river are still.

Psalm 26 (a)

try my conscience

Try my conscience free for ninety days
and if not satisfied receive your money
back, but of course you keep the conscience.
As you can see, I've tried a hundred ways
to rid myself of this anomaly
of self, this messenger of God's vengeance.
If we were meant to know the difference
of right from wrong we wouldn't have a heart
and I'm not so sure we'd have common sense.
Try to tell wisdom and common sense apart.
Try to tell the heart what to feel, or how
hard to feel it. Try to tell then from now
without a crystal ball. Do what is good:
it's another thing to do what will be good.

Psalm 26 (b)

Assay my conscience as a miner tries
a spoon of gold by melting it and skimming
off the dross—or as a doctor assays
the kidney, sieving its limpidity
of blood. The conscience is in the kidney
for the writers of the Psalms; so I pray
the Lord to look a light through my conscience
and see if it escapes me clean and pure,
as clean as the river of dreams that gladdens
the City of God. Let clearly appear
the last analysis, better or worse.
The Talmud says that we don't see the world
as it is; we see the world that we are.
God's City is peace, but we are at war.

Psalm 26 (c)

Let me not rest with the self-deceived,
suffer not my friends to sit with a liar:
don't let me accept what I want to believe;
if everything's dire, well, let it be dire.
There once was a man who sang in a choir,
made notes through his nose, and sang with a snore.
Whenever the melody tried to go higher
he crumpled his music, he grumbled, he swore.
At last came the day when the sexton objected,
had words with the vicar, director, and more,
but the fellow, elected, would not be corrected,
divested his vesture and stormed out the door.
Indignance abounding, not seeing surroundings,
he strayed toward the street and was hit by a bus.
Let this be a lesson, confounding, astounding:
if we are that fellow, it would have been us.

Psalm 27

The Lord is my light and my salvation

My enemies still try to swallow me,
take me to court again, cool hypocrites,
maneuvering—blind dogs that follow me
into the alley where I lie, dump shit
on my painful head and trot off howling
in the moonlight, sanctimonious as—
bloodhounds, divorcees, the dead; I don't know—
but I am on a rock like Alcatraz,
full of vision of the Lord: I see light
and salvation; I see the Lord's beauty;
I see Jesus coming robed in pure white—
the everlasting angel company—
mother and father and the pearly host—
peace, Soul—the living, many-splendored Ghost!

Psalm 28
if thou be silent

If thou be silent, the pine wind would fall
along the river like glass; fatty clouds
would slide like milk down emphysemic walls
of dirty air. No it would not be good.
We would lose our feel for sound: our noises
would become visible, because vision
is the residual torture—no one chooses
blindness over other sense excisions.
But if the silence were yours and not ours,
what of the universe would not go dead?
What would separate all the even hours?
Is not "Let there be light" still being said?
If thou be silent, that crow would take root,
black under the shadowy branch, and mute.

Psalm 30 (a)
Sing unto the Lord

But the voice of the Lord is upon the waters,
upon the waters we call nothingness,
upon the void, slate of the universe:
it hews and shapes the burgeoning excess,
waste, of shimmering violet, red, blue
hydrogen processing from dust to dust—
startled by commands beautiful and cruel
like a captive, reverent Canaanite host.
The voice of the Lord thunders from mountains
and sweeps valleys clean; its lightning lays bare
green-robed trees—vine-twining sun-drawn virgins—
with gold, rolling, raptor-legged huge-voiced fire.
Above, in the beauty of holiness,
the temple of the Lord spreads in silence.

Psalm 30 (b)

O Lord my God, I will give thanks
unto thee for ever

And I extol thee, Lord of mountain thunder,
sounds of running water and running feet
of children, the sudden feathery plunge
of eagle—discursive crow—the thin bleed
of dreamers' sighs. To you alone I cried,
and you have raised me up to sing, to give
thanks by sounding out praise; you give these eyes
words, fingers syllables, breath time: to live
is to answer. I say thanks while I can.
I know there is silence hovering over
me and the grave is a quiet place. Then
will your hand rise and your command enrobe
our unsensed souls with the sound of your voice?
Or will you speak to us like ghost to ghost,
silent as an imagined universe?

Psalm 30 (c)
Thou hast lifted me up

You lifted me up like water from a deep well;
or as a strong man bends from a stout boat,
grips the arms of an exhausted man, pulls
him streaming, gasping up, lays him out
across a bench, so did you pull me out—
a dead weight; and you touched me: I was healed
of the earth, healed of its depths of waters,
of its weight of waters, healed of its stone,
healed of the fissures and salt of its wounds,
healed of what the children of men have done;
I was healed of night. I went down to bed
and suffered in Your arms, dry and old and worn
like a dead root; you held me until morning
came up—and look at me, raised from the dead.

Psalm 30 (d)

for His anger endureth but a moment

All right, admit the Lord is angry now
and then—a crash of expletives, a lash
across the face with His belt, maybe Pow!
with His fist, maybe a razor-sharp gash
or two across the face and a quick
trip to the emergency room for stitches,
stay at home a few days while the bruises
fade—once there was this dislocated shoulder
when He twisted your arm: we all lose
control now and then. Don't overrate control:
you want a God who's living, after all;
and before you complain, uselessly, think
what other people get: AIDS, rape, lupus.
Poor people with nothing to eat or drink.
We are His. Why should he try to please us?
Think of what He did to Jesus. Praise him.

Psalm 30 (e)

Sing unto the Lord, O ye saints of His

There is no wrath of God,
 only the wrath of Man.
The testament of blood
 reveals what is divine.

Behold the Lamb of God,
 the Holy One in dust—
divinely free and good;
 pure, innocent, and just.

Indifferent is the sod,
 indifferent is the sand:
there is no wrath of God,
 only the wrath of Man.

Psalm 31

My times are in your hand

1

"Design," a poet asked—for human life—
does design "govern in a thing so small"?
Grand or minute, is there a plan at all?
Is the cosmos a grandiose trifle
at best watched by some stupendous indifference—
a macroeconomic Zen; at worst
entertainment for the gods, *tour de force*?
Or nothing really, governed by flat chance?
No claim of meaning can mean anything:
there are always higher points of reference.
If there's meaning for God, what does God mean?
Who asks? A trapped, self-reflective being
inhaling the smoke of his burning senses?
The knife of reason always comes out clean.

2

The question has been asked so many times.
We are afraid, and poetry is dust.
Perhaps we ask simply because we must:
what we call freedom is mere choice of rhymes.
Whether one is inevitable simply
doesn't matter. What if it weren't? One rhyme
did not have to be sounded: this one time
no laws applied, no cause stated or implied.
Talk about meaningless. A dog barks nearby,
bearing the universe on its hoarse praise,
comprehending what a dog comprehends,
wise the way only a dog can be wise,
understanding with its soft nose the ways
of God; smiling, or panting, at its fence.

Psalm 32 (a)

I will instruct you

Go forward; I will show you where to go.
If I say, "Into that quicksand"—but then,
I wouldn't say that, would I? Would you know
that I was joking, testing maybe? Pen
in hand, you write whatever's in your head,
assuming it was I who inspired you—
questions, sarcasm, despair, hope: I said
it all. *Where my spirit lives and moves,*
there shall you follow, little one, my own.
Where did that come from? *Lift up your heart;*
rise up and walk: you are my daughter, son,
dust of dust and light of light. Where you are,
there am I. Is anything outside you?
(Thou hast redeemed me, O Lord God of truth.)

Psalm 32 (b)

Happy is one whose sins are forgiven

I wish I knew. I wish I knew the sins,
and wish I knew if I were done with them,
and wish I knew the wrath of God is meant
for someone else. My live Hitler within—
I want to meet him, little by little
preferably—the child in *Lederhosen*,
the fidgeting young corporal posing
for a struggle, the dwarf inner Yiddish
speaking backwards like an incantation,
the thick black ink spreading like a nation.
He ate his last meal knowing it was last—
ladled it up like an old man—good food—
his head bending toward the mouthed pistol blast.
King of the Jews, pity me as I do!

Psalm 33 (a)

By the word of the Lord were the heavens made

He spoke, and behold, it was done—the mass
of matter, black and light, unseen and seen.
The universe God knows is hidden,
by far most of it, from the likes of us,
but so it is: what words accomplish, blessing
and curse, ducks beneath our knowledge, stays down
while our instruments and sovereign reason
pass over, and goes about its business.
God could make a universe with a few
choice words: a little bit of talk and Bang!
turnips on the kitchen table. What you
and I could do with a little tight slang
slung across a deep, if we could find one:
here an earth with sin and death, there a sun.

Psalm 33 (b)
Blessed is the nation whose God is the Lord

"This nation, or any nation so conceived"?
The writer of the Psalm meant Israel,
so may we make a claim on God as well?
But how much can God be asked to believe?
In Hitler's army every soldier wore
a buckle stamped, bold-lettered, "GOD WITH US."
Our dollar's printed with "in God we trust."
And so it goes for every buck and war—
for God's in everything and nothing all
at once: we all can ask the good Lord's grace;
we can be wrong. History is God's face
seen by the blind. "The will of God prevails"
in consequences. Blessed is the nation
not quite sure of its salvation.

Psalm 34

The Lord is near to the broken-hearted

"This poor man cried," and somehow, though the earth
is lost among the strange nights of time
a hundred billion galaxies deep, winding
around a consciousness and living heart
aware of all at once, living in all
the way a sparrow's terror flutters
in your hand—although there is no bottom
or outer reach to despair—when I called,
You were there, as close as the soul, solid
as a thought on the ice of nothingness,
here. You answer me. The homely fragrance
of roasting corn on the summer air rides
eons out. Sorrow—the great whale of space—
is nothing but passion, nothing but grace.

Psalm 35 (a)

Let their way be dark and slippery; and let the angel of the Lord pursue them.

But on the other hand, my enemies
are right: I am the criminal they say
I am, and worse. Just let the light of day
fall on my attitude, my perfidies,
and what, through thinking only of myself,
I've done to other people—how I've changed
their lives, not for the better, before I
would change my own for their sakes. I swore I
would obey the Commandments; I explain
my Sherman's march through them all to myself
plausibly somehow—doesn't matter how—
and go on my merry way—well not now
so merry. An enemy of myself.

Psalm 35 (b)

*Let their way be dark and slippery; and let
the angel of the Lord pursue them.*

Were I to see myself the way God sees,
I would probably commit suicide.
This is no joke, nor is it poetry,
nor is it some kind of smug, humble pride
(yes, I repeat I know it's not poetry)
in self-abnegation: me satisfied
somehow by confession, me my own priest—
the lie of self-righteousness, then the lie
in doggerel, for that is what this is—
one lie after another until I
die; and on the other hand I crave sight,
the ability to know a good rhyme
when I see it—a perfect, holy crime.

Psalm 36

in Your light shall we see light

1

"God of God and Light of Light, very God
of very God": these words, so beautiful,
belong less in a creed than in a heart.
More poetry and deed than you are thought,
you, words, are the very stuff of the Word
that made and ordered everything, even
now the breath in life, even now the Alpha
and Omega spelling out the *alma
redemptoris mater*—the Word of heaven—
through all languages one—Who made and was,
is, and ever shall be: together one.
Mother, Father, Son—each the living cause
of the other: but here on earth the Son—
in your light shall we see light—beautiful—
spoken syllable of the Only One.

2

It could be plainer. Language need not be
a hymn, ecstatic, incomprehensible.
It could simply state the facts. If there are any.
The Christian creeds might be defensible.
You ask a simple question, "who is Jesus?"
The answer is even simpler: He is God.
That's what we call God around here: Jesus.
"Wait a minute, not so fast," you say. "God
is Jesus?" No, the creeds say it's the other
way around. All the difference in the world.
That's why we call them Parent, Child.
That's the point of Jesus having a mother.
"I think I'll stick with poetry," you say.
"And Jesus didn't help when he was here:
he said he was the Light, the Truth, the Way;
one with the Father, I AM. Poetry."
But "you," of course, are only on this page—
as I am, writing you, both of us one
like father, son. So it is that Reason
gets out of hand fast, like a sonnet gone
to seed—perfectly good rhymes get buried
in flat chatter—images turn into
ideas, and it's all basically prose.
What we want to know, no-one really knows.
Certainty is bliss, but it is sin, too.

Psalm 37
the meek shall inherit the earth

1

How long, O Lord, how long shall we deceive
ourselves? The meek (read: the poor) die like shad,
praying emaciated on the banks
of the sacred Ganges, or dried brown leaves
to sweep up from the streets of Calcutta.
Dead dreams under knit caps in schizophrenic
heads and thin prostitutes a century
from home on the streets of Philadelphia—
the meek, the poor, the innocent and pure,
the dreams nobody dreams any more,
the consumed, the raped, the beaten, the shot:
enough already—the Jews in their ovens—
enough, enough: a single drop refutes
a leather bibleful of heavens.

2

And yet—there must be an "and yet" to meekness
meaning only a mouthful of worms,
because religion is only human
and the claim was resurrected by Jesus
in full knowledge of its timely demise
at the hands of the prophet Job—in full
view of the hungry, the poor, and of all
the doomed Jews with names written in the skies.
He pushed the old sentence into our teeth,
and others like it one after another,
blessings full of irony and murder,
blatantly false, a sower throwing seeds
on good graveyard soil, knowing what it yields:
the blood of martyrs, lilies of the fields.

Psalm 38

Forsake me not

The trees stand in that late summer stillness,
those high firs and balsams a little gray.
Mornings are quieter too. Few birds stay
in this dry back yard long. Bushes are brittle
and spiny; their branches are no longer
young. I am tired of summer. The garden
is pretty small this year, unwatered, not
interesting, just a disappointment.
Those sort of hazy high clouds, sitting far
up and across half the sky, make it neither
cloudy nor bright, and I know the still air
gets more and more polluted. The damn flies bite
but no rain is coming. I stand at night
outside. Summer Triangle is still there.

Psalm 39

*O Lord, remove thy stroke from me . . . for I
am a stranger with thee, and a sojourner,
as all my fathers were.*

My father lay in silence for two months,
unconscious while a restless succession
of old men with heart attacks, operations,
minor strokes were carried in one by one
like firewood in flimsy cotton nightshirts,
knobby knees and saddle hips almost bare
through late summer, early fall—TV blaring,
sitting up for Jell-o, stubble-chinned flirts
and hollow snorers, wheeled out one by one
more well than they would ever be again,
while he lay there comatose. He had been,
well, a physician, musician, a man.
One day when I came in his eyes were open—
body, heart, life, everything but gaze, broken.

*O Lord, remove thy stroke from me . . . for I
am a stranger with thee, and a sojourner,
as all my fathers were.*

Psalm 40

he hath put a new song in my mouth
(at the death of Senator Edward Kennedy)

The trumpet falls on the late, perishing
air; the muffled drums tap for the last time
in our lives: the last brave brother has died.
What dream, without them, are we cherishing?
They wrote poetry in this people's heart,
gave a cadence to compassion. Vision
climbed stairs of lyric speech. This saved nation
would play the ancient rage of human doubt
without its romantics, its pilgrim great.
From the manor to earth like banners furled
by the tough aristocracy of fate—
self-evidently just, to dust returned—
clarion heralds of a newer world:
and the perishing hearts within us burned.

Psalm 41

Blessed is the one who considers the poor

"How we suffer," say the poor; "how we struggle."
Yet boundaries there must be: did not God
Himself set bounds to day and night, then made
the world? Reality might be ugly
but there is no other game in town.
In another world and time, another
mind, the Angel of the Lord passes over
all whose doorposts run with the blood of lambs:
but here, Reality, the only game
in town, the Angel of the Living God
stays only for a time the cosmic rage,
the flaming revolutionary sword,
lays in the lovely blessing of a Bible verse
the merciful, just, and inevitable curse.

Psalm 42 (a)

As the hart panteth after the water brooks,
so panteth my soul after thee, O God.

To long for God is life. For this the world
exists; the universe bleeds out its wrathful
agony in blood so forced it is hurled
into light; and dark matter's gravity
wanders into itself like a starving
body. I thirst! The Son of Man, living
water himself, thirsts to crucifixion.
"There is no God in our heaven"—
no presence by vision or intinction:
that is to long and yearn like murder
in the bones, mere quantum physics carving
existence out of nothing but words.
Why art thou disquieted, O my soul?—
for this you were made: thirst, yearning, death, hope.

Psalm 42 (b)

thy billows are gone over me
(the burial of Edward Kennedy)

One's failings, he said, no more than one's sorrows,
no more than disasters, provide excuses
for quitting. No mistake replaces duty;
no loss lessens obligation to do
for others what they cannot do. The rich,
he said, can take care of themselves; the poor
must have help. They are a nation's measure:
they weigh the country's dream. Today the torch
in darkness dims far off. Our old heroes'
voices are still. Who will speak for the poor;
who will light, lift, and lead the rest of us—
show us how to take it and how to dare?
It is for Lincoln's children to be consecrated:
it is for us, the living, to be dedicated.

Psalm 43

*Judge me, O God, and plead my cause
against an ungodly nation*

My generation's heroes seemed to fight
their own beloved country. Some were killed
for self-evident truths—for an old bill
of rights: equality in law; the rights
to live, speak, write, pray, and simply to eat,
and to be handled graciously when ill;
and for demanding that we do as well
by other nations as our own. And yet
their brothers rose against them in the name
of God and nation—sanctimonious
and smug as reptiles, ostentatiously sane,
rigidly righteous, certain to the bone,
jealous for an angel's reputation.
Save us, O God, from a godly nation.

*Judge me, O God, and plead my cause
against an ungodly nation*

It doesn't mean that God is somewhere else,
for no such place exists: "ungodly" means
being liberal in designer jeans,
a little north of young and south of svelt;
it means feeding your children refried beans
and carrying a card that's not the green
of money; thinking money is called "gelt,"
in fact (since "ethnic" really means "obscene");
not living where the Sunday streets are clean,
and coming from somewhere below the belt—
the Bible Belt, that is, where black Ruths glean
the cotton fields in antebellum dreams,
old time religion saves the saved from hell,
and Adam never multiplied, or fell.

Psalm 44

Why do you hide your face?

The meek, the powerless, the sloppy poor
who shop for junk in tee shirts and used pants,
who lay down their self-respect at the door
and come into waiting rooms like supplicants—
have they been unfaithful, Lord?—forgotten
You as they mumbled down the streets, neglected
prayers, thanksgivings, praise in their forgotten
alleys; have they taken You for granted
while we carried on the business of this
world, no thanks to them, no thanks to their quiet
and ignorant beggar children, their Christian
dreams of youth, their long tuberculosis,
their Mexican carbohydrate diet?
Why do You hide Your hungry face from us?

Psalm 45

forget also thine own people

For this man is your master: you bow down
to him, this graceful man whose sword is business—
he can afford you. Your town in Thailand
can do without one more poor girl, a dress
meant by a mother for something less final,
shoes destined for the night streets of Bangkok—
and maybe your mother will make more girls.
And forget your father, forget his talk,
his brave talk, about prospering and buying
you back. What god does not favor this man
in the silk suit? He is almost divine
already: from Great Britain to Japan
they know him, love him, wholeheartedly trust
him, and they submit to him, as you must.

Psalm 46 (a)

God is our refuge

The final place, the final resting place—
but God is restless, forever moving
while at rest, still creating as if space
were endless—judging, forgiving, renewing
us as though you and I were infinities:
the origin and goal of beauty, all
in all in One, and there is no place
where we are unsafe. The gates of hell fall,
our unlived lives come home, everything is born;
across the last field imagination
raises his arms afar like the loving
brother Esau—rich, powerful, ours
more than breath, faithfully and kindly moving
toward us grand and sure as our final hour.

Psalm 46 (b)

There is a river

No stream runs through Jerusalem, no stream
makes glad any of the earth's sad cities.
We are past being glad. What we all see
is rising oceans, sky you cannot breathe,
and booted men like locusts. What we need
is planet Earth the way it used to be,
blue that is blue and green that is real green—
water clear as justice, spirits in the trees.
Somewhere in the great beyond, somewhere soon,
you can be a child. You can be in love.
You can rest on a summer afternoon.
You can talk to an angel. You can believe.
There is a river beside you, just look:
your shoes, the pen that you left, and your book.

Psalm 47
clap your hands, all ye people

Give it up for the Lord. The world's a stage
and He plays all the parts, including this,
the TV preacher with the spider kiss,
the Bible-thumper who is all the rage—
a pacing cliché, including his lust
for organists, gullible widows, boys,
expensive cars, or political toys—
whatever's worst, and whatever he must.
Is He creating us, the thoughtful ones—
looking out at us into the spotlights,
greasepaint on his ancient face, wearing tights,
rolling starry eyes and cheeking His tongue—
while sitting in the cheap seats looking on,
Holy Ghost, Father, disconcerted Son?

Psalm 48

he will be our guide, even unto death

We shall not die alone. The ones who love
us and have gone before shall welcome us
like early rain on high summer meadows,
open their arms to us: and our Jesus
if the child in us believed him; or Mary
if she was our heart's devotion; Krishna
if the blue of his cool heaven clothed us;
or the Maiden of the Mountains, her hair
braided with a golden eagle feather—
so shall the Old One, the Everlasting,
walk the Ghost Road with us, calming and strong
beside us, the pacing wolf, the shepherd
of our souls, the Innermost—at our death,
the hour of our death, when the dear Lord
touches our brave face and becomes our breath.

Psalm 49

he shall receive me

This pathos is depression of the mind,
this sense that seems like clear perception: sadness
of life—the earnest and well-meaning child
who spends her last money on some small gladness;
the gracious artful one who trusts only
being alone; the wondering bright boy
who'll never understand what he did wrong;
the dreaming in the dark, and the kind soul.
Surely this is not how it really is.
Someone sees it differently; someone knows
pain mathematically, a physicist
with a crown of thorns, a mystical rose
of comprehension who is sadness born,
and joy in our own sacrificial form.

Psalm 50

Our God shall come, and shall not keep silence:
a fire shall devour before him . . .

Anna

You should have been an autumn visitor
ordained amid the golden, red, and orange
décor of late October for terror,
or maybe humor: you should have been born
somewhere else and another time. You should
a lot of things. Should not be mentally
disturbed, should not be in this neighborhood,
should have the drive and enterprise to rally.
Should not be hook-nosed, with three rotten teeth,
pushing your shopping cart through supermarkets
like this, all your clothes in bags no doubt reeking
of who knows what and why. But here you are.
It would be much better if you weren't poor.

It is winter now and you sleep outdoors,
God knows where and how. You wear an old coat,
quilted but thin, witch-black, and brush the floor
with ragged black sweatpants. Around your throat
is no scarf and you seem to have no gloves.
All you have is piled in your cart, as if
anyone would steal what little you have.
Your scraggly steel hair would attract notice
but I don't want to look up and embarrass
you. Wouldn't children be afraid, and ask
obvious and blatant questions? Someone
should do something—rather do something more
than Social Services probably does.

They are always with us—I mean the poor.
I wonder what the ugliest person
I have ever seen buys. But this author
doesn't want her to feel shame; I go on
with my food gathering and forget her
until she pulls behind me at check-out.
With the curiosity of compassion
I see she has some boxes of prepared
food. Tactful, I pay, leave. I am an asshole.
I should have paid her bill. I wasn't scared;
I just didn't think. When they come to get
the ashes of the Jews I never noticed
at Belsen, I'll be standing at the door

of one of the ovens. The crematoria
are still warm. I'll feel sorry for the angels
who have to do the work; and it is sure
I'd ask if there's anything I can do.
But what if those dread Visitors are sane?
My point is: when it dips below zero
like last night, where does she find enough warmth
to survive? To the pure, all things are pure.
This is not about me; it's about her
and it's about the Earth, hot at the core;
and if there is really sin, does it burn
the way innocence burns? What has she done?
Why was Jesus so in love with the poor?

If this woman, Anna, came to my door—
"Why?" is what I'd rather ask: "Why, O Lord,
is there injustice, poverty, and tightness
of heart? If the fault is ours, it is Yours;
and if You can change the world, so can we."
But what if she came to my door some night—
the wind howling, shadows dancing, black branches
clacking, candles in Jack-O-Lanterns snapping,
goblins slipping between the shrubbery,
the Eve of All Saints, witches and devils
howling in the distance coming closer?
Would she remind me I can pay her bill
still, by asking what my spare room is for?

And let's say the time is twelve-o-four.
The ghosts are gone; it's All Saints Day at last,
with a few minutes to spare. I am cold—
I am always cold; I wish I were ague-
proof, but at least there's no-one at the door
any more, though her looped and windowed, ragged
costume might be enough to keep me warm.
Police found a frozen woman this morning
(it isn't really All Saints, but much later)
under newspapers in hollowed-out snow
(dead because we're sick, and we hated her),
outside some asshole's decorated door.
She will be cremated, paid by the State,
our taxes once again warming the poor.

Psalm 50

I am God, even thy God.

In this word is silence, and in this silence
vision: an old woman carefully spooning
her soup, little bowl in a trembling hand
and spoon in a fist like an infant's tool.
She sits hunched in lonely concentration,
stunned by the roundness of her memories,
her coin purse on the table in the sun,
cane hooked on the chair's arm; and what she sees
when she looks up is young people. Talking
couples walk by and I stare at the holy
ghost of her soul. She is already all
right; in her is the knower and the known.
Dear One, I salute in you the sunrise.
I no longer fear the vast galaxies.

www.ingramcontent.com/pod-product-compliance
Lightning Source LLC
Chambersburg PA
CBHW072010090426
42734CB00033B/2327

Index

- Foreword & Our Story — 1
- How to use this book — 6
- Questionnaire — 8
- Stress — 17
- Ambiance — 21
- Conversation Starters — 23
- Craft — 27
- DVD — 30
- Games — 33
- Gardening — 37
- Gifts — 40
- Internet — 42
- Legals — 48
- Manipulation & Tactile — 50
- Music — 53
- Oral History — 60
- Personal Care — 64
- Photos — 67
- Physical Activities — 70
- Reading — 73
- Religion — 76
- Sport — 78
- Technology — 80
- Travel — 88
- TV shows & Movies — 89
- Conclusion — 92

Aged & Engaged
www.agedandengaged.com

Foreword

This book has come about from the experience we had as a family, when we had a Loved One – our mother/grandma who went from an independent lifestyle to gradually having to live with fulltime high care assistance.

We really wanted to do something to help keep our Loved One engaged with the world – but we didn't know how to go about it. What was out there for us?

While our experience has been with an aging family member, in researching material for this book it has become very obvious to us that people needing assisted living can range across all ages. Therefore throughout the book when we refer to Loved Ones, we are referring to anyone gone from independent living to any kind of assisted living or care.   We use the word loved as we believe that if you are reading this book then you have someone in mind who you love, be they family or friend.

This isn't a medical book, or a book specifically targeting dementia or Alzheimer's disease. It won't help you to find suitable aged care, a nursing care facility, respite or at home care. What it will do, is provide you with ideas to keep your loved one stimulated and feeling a part of life. It's about quality of life for both your loved one and you as a family.

It is a very stressful time, both for the person going through the change in lifestyle and also the family who are there to support them.

The pace of life today is hectic for everyone and having loved ones who may need that extra assistance, be they parents, partner, grandparents or friends, is becoming a reality for us all.

Our story

Our own experience and the reason for this book, is the story of our loved one - Nanna, Yole Jones.

On 1st August 2012, Nanna, who had lived next door to us in an extended family situation for 32 years, had a stroke. All of our lives were turned upside down.

Up until this stage Nanna was living semi-independently. She would go to the local club to meet up with friends and was line dancing until she was 85-years-old. As it became harder for her to drive herself, she became more reliant on others to assist.

Being of strong Italian stock, this loss of independence was difficult for her to accept and we experienced firsthand her moods of loneliness, sadness and anger. Typically, these feelings were often projected onto closest family.

Fortunately, we lived close by and could keep an eye on her, a privilege a lot of families do not have. We now understand the worry, fear and sometimes, guilt that a lot of people experience when they can't see their loved ones on a regular basis.

After Yole's stroke, it became apparent that she could no longer return home. She was to be sent from the hospital to a transitional facility in a building reminiscent of the hospitals of the 1950s, with four people in a room. Because of her stroke, Yole wasn't able to walk, toilet herself or converse clearly.

This was a very stressful time for our family. What could we do? We had just two weeks to make our applications and we put Yole's name on six lists for a permanent nursing home bed. We wanted to see what was on offer and choose the best. Luckily, our jobs allowed us to take extended time off work, a luxury many families do not have and they have to engage Nursing Home Brokers to do this for them.

We were suddenly immersed in the world of nursing home bonds, unbonded placements, assets tests, Centre Link (the Australian government agency which handles pensions and social services entitlements), daily nursing care fees, ACAT assessment and enduring powers of attorney. This was an incredibly stressful time for the whole family with masses of forms to fill in, decisions to make and endless paperwork.

Finally, due to a combination of research and good luck, we were offered a place for Nanna at a lovely facility. We then had to find a $250,000 bond – not an easy task for any family. It required the marketing and selling of her house which we were given six months to do.

Again this was very stressful; the house had a lot of history and attachment. It wasn't easy to manage the sale in such a short time frame and in a depressed market.

Once Nanna was settled, it didn't get much easier for the family as we watched her become bedbound and needing a fall out chair. Despite the pleasant surroundings and terrific staff, her limited independence and now failing ability to communicate meant that she was often lonely and sad.

What could we do to lift her spirits? Like many families, we had the best of intentions but were time poor and could not get to see her every day. We shared the visits between ourselves but then didn't quite know what to do when we got there. It is a powerless feeling.

As a family, we decided there must be something we could do and between us came up with a number of ideas. Could we get a DVD on "line dancing", get her pictures made into a book that she could flip through, put the pictures on a DVD that would run in a loop, convert some of her pictures into a 12 piece jigsaw puzzle? We sourced special pictures that could be placed onto the walls to look like window scenes to bring the outside world in.

We found outlets where you could find tactile activities so she could touch various textures stimulating all the senses and provide ideas for people who visited her, about what they could talk to her about. We found TV and DVD sets with one remote control (a real challenge) and incredible technology that is out there to assist families monitor and keep contact from a distance.

We sourced DVDs and books on places she had travelled and how to make a mobile garden that could be taken in to her bedside. We found diversional therapy ideas and products that are available to the professionals in the industry which could also be used by families. We found ideas for presents for birthdays, Christmas and special occasions. We found lots of ideas, which we believe could assist in keeping the aged engaged; ideas that form the basis of this book, our website, blogs, forums and consultancy services.

In this book we use the term "loved ones" again we are referring to anyone regardless of age who has or is moving from independent living to any kind of assisted living or care.   These people may be partners, parents, grandparents or friends. They may live in the family home, by themselves, in a granny flat out the back, a retirement village or in a high care nursing home.

We do hope you get ideas to help your loved ones get the most out of their later lives and suggestions that will make you feel that you are really helping them stay involved and engaged so that they have great quality of life.

About Mindworks and Aged & Engaged

Aged and Engaged is happy to be associated with Mindworks Australasia Pty Ltd who have been a leading Corporate Training company in Australia since 1987.

Laurie Kelly, the director of Mindworks, specialises in Brain Friendly Training and the mysteries of the Mind. He works with individuals and corporate groups on how they might utilise their mind(s) and their potential. With our own family story related elsewhere, he and his family have become immersed into the world of caring for a loved family elder (our Nanna) who went from independent living to dependent care and all the turmoil that brings.

We have included throughout this book ideas which we believe are both practical and brain friendly to maximise the opportunities for engagement and the passion of a great quality of life.

If you have any questions or wish to discuss any ideas or issues discussed within this book, please feel free to contact us.

website - www.agedandengaged.com
email - info@agedandengaged.com

How to use this book

To get the best value out of this book we would suggest that you begin by filling out the questionnaire preferably with your loved one's involvement or others who have been close to them throughout their lives. You will notice the layout is designed so that you can take notes, write ideas and share with others so that you get the most out of this book.

- The questionnaire will help you focus on your loved one and their needs. In times of stress we sometimes forget little things which can be very important. This questionnaire is the one that we use within our consultancy service to help us map out the best individual package of recommendations and products for families who initially find it difficult to source these things themselves.

- Look through the ideas around each topic under chapter headings. These ideas will stimulate your thinking and give you practical suggestions on what you might be able to do. Don't get overwhelmed by the volume of ideas within this book and on our webpage, just start with simple ideas which are both fun for your loved one and you.

We have highlighted throughout the book some "quick win" ideas which can be quickly and simply implemented to have an immediate and real impact.

Links and up to date information on all products/resources mentioned within the book can be found at our website www.agedandengaged.com.au.

Current research indicates that social interaction is a very powerful way to keep people engaged with life. The majority of ideas within this book promote and help to increased social interaction with family/friends.

The book is a dynamic resource, meant to be shared with your network of friends and family. Please come and join our extended family, where you can get updated with information and ideas or share your own story and successes. The more ideas that are shared the more beneficial these resources will be for us all.

Website - www.agedandengaged.com
Facebook – www.facebook.com/agedandengaged

We also offer a consultancy service for those of you who are time poor or where distance/location may be an issue. Don't be embarrassed or feel guilty. We can help.

Remember: Just keep it simple and have
             . fun with your loved one.

Questionnaire

The questionnaire will help you focus on your loved one and what their needs are, in times of stress we sometimes forget little things which can be very important.   This questionnaire is the one that we use within our consultancy service to help us map out the best individual package of recommendations and products for families who initially find it difficult to source these things themselves.

Some questions may appear to be obvious to family members like 'marital status' but by consciously writing them down, it will help trigger your own thinking and memories, which can be very important as you use the ideas in this book.

The Basics

1, Full Name _____

2, Date of birth / age _____

3, Place of birth _____

4, Marital status _____

5, Does your loved one have any children, grandchildren or great grandchildren?

6, Do they see them regularly?

7, Are there challenges in this area?

8, What are their family traditions?

9, Can they be continued and to what extent?

10, To help you identify ideas around family, briefly write down how important family is to them and some background information.

11, Is your loved one living at home or in residential care?

12, If in residential care, is it high or low care?

13, If at home, what sort of care is provided, if any, from within the family or by support services like Home Help or Meals on Wheels?

14, Brief history of their medical condition and anything that may be limiting their physical or mental capacity.

15, If your loved one is bedridden, is there anything they are able to do independently now?

16, Does your loved one have things they can manipulate and touch to keep their senses active?

Sport

17, What sports did they play or enjoy throughout their lifetime?
For example:

- Bowls
- Tennis
- Football
- NRL/Rugby /AFL
- Golf
- Horse racing
- Netball
- Surfing
- Sailing
- Cricket
- Fishing
- Dancing
- Other……………..

18, How physically active are they now?

19, Are there limitations to the physical activities they can engage in now?

Music

20, What is their taste in music?

Vintage
- 40s
- 50s
- 60s

Type
- Sing-a-long
- Vaudeville
- Dance
- Classic
- Jazz
- Folk
- Country
- Other……………..

Gardening

21, Were, or are, they keen gardeners? What sort of gardening did they do or have?

- Flowers
- Landscaping
- Fruit and vegetables

Travel

22, Did they enjoy travel throughout their life?

23, What countries have they traveled to, or possibly have lived in?

Places Travelled
- Australia
- Africa
- Asia
- Europe
- American & Canada
- South America
- Pacific
- Other……………..

TV & Movies

24, Television programs they like or have liked.

25, To help source suitable DVDs for them it is important that you reflect on the types of programs they enjoy or enjoyed.

Hobbies

26, There are a lot of suggestions that can be made for hobbies. Firstly, you need to identify what your loved one used to like doing and their capacity now to engage in these interests. For example:
- Cooking
- Craft
- Machinery
- Woodwork
- Other……………..

Reading

27, There are a lot of useful ideas for people who like books and reading in the following chapters. However, can we suggest that you think through the type of reading your loved one enjoyed:

Type of books
- Fiction
- Drama
- Romance
- Mystery
- Historical
- Science fiction
- Autobiographical
- Other……………..

Games

28, Games and card players. Were they card players and if so what sort? Canasta, Five Hundred, Bridge, Mahjong, Poker, Euchre or Rummican?

29, Did your loved one enjoy playing board games and do they have any favourites?

30, Crosswords, Scrabble, Sudoku? Playing the pokies?

Photos

31, What sort of photo collections does your loved one have?

32, Can they be grouped into different times in their lives?

Technology

33, Are they familiar at all with computers/tablets?

34, What sort of technology are they using, if any?

35, Are they willing to learn how to use technologies like tablets or iPads with simple apps?

Religious Affiliations

36, What are your loved ones beliefs?

37, Is this currently an important part of their life or was it in their past?

Other engaging ideas or interests

38, Anything else you can think of that might help with sourcing different ideas to keep your loved one engaged?

Other issues of important note

39, Is there anything else that comes to mind that is important to your loved one?

Stress

Be in no doubt, as our love ones become older and need support at home and in nursing care it can become a very stressful time for everyone. It is stressful for you, as the support people, and it is a stressful time for them.

A new world of the unknown.

For many of us it can come as a shock (especially sudden severe illness), a sense that everything as we have known has changed or is about to change. We suddenly experience a sense of loss, a grieving for what was and a fear of what is about to be. We enter a world of medical, legal and government red-tape, possibly a time to find new living arrangements, face decisions about the sale or rental of family homes etc etc. and all too often this has to be done quickly. Add to this a sense of bewilderment and a sense of powerlessness.

Hopefully the ideas in this book will give you some practical things that you can do to keep your loved one engaged throughout this latter stage of their lives. These ideas are meant to reduce the sense of powerlessness, to provide you with actions and ideas aimed at keep your loved ones mentally and physically engaged with life.

This being said here are some ideas to help with your stress and to help your loved one cope with their stress.

STRESS

There are many other well written books on Stress and Stress management which we are not going to quote and re-write for you as they are readily available as are tapes and video programs. It is however worth considering that for all of us when we are stressed the chemical Cortisol is produced in the brain to help us recognise danger and cope with it. This is terrific when the branch laying across the bush track ahead of us begins to move and we instantly know this is not good news. The adrenaline chemical in our brain then kicks in and we go into flight mode. These chemicals are vital for our well being. However too much of them can cause physical reaction in our body and thinking.

Too much Cortisol can lead to confusion, inability to think clearly, loss of short term memory and a sense of being overwhelmed and powerlessness.

These are symptoms which carers and older loved ones both experience.

Stress & the Carer:

As mentioned above and throughout the book this could well be one of the most stressful times in your life. If you are going to be the best possible carer you would like to be, you become the priority. If you do not look after yourself during this period you will not be in a good condition to care for your loved one.

Stress for your Loved One:

Believe it or not your aging loved one will be dealing with a lot of stress as well, as they think about their circumstances. They will be worried that their short term memory is not as good as it once was, how they will handle life as they get frailer, what happens if they get sick, old friends are beginning to pass, will they be able to stay in their family home, what happens if their partner is sick, what if they lose their licence and who will help them. Do they look sad selling their home and moving into a retirement village. What are their options? Often they will not want to worry family members or be a burben and in the process create a daily life of worry for themselves as these ideas dwell on their minds. If they are in nursing care they will often go through a sense of despair and powerlessness. What is the use??? The thoughts about life and death can also be a big concern.

IDEAS

- You are not superhuman. You can only do what you can do!

- Guilt is a wasted emotion. Positive forward movement is what is needed.

- Enlist help from family and friends to implement some of the ideas in this book. Don't be the hero.

    - Set up a social media page for the support network so everyone can see what is happening, adding the activities and success they have had when they visited or called on the telephone.
    - There are so many support groups out there as explained in this book from Meals on Wheels, Home Assist, government support for cleaning and weekly shopping trips and so many volunteer groups out there in nearly every area. Get onto the local G.P. Library Council or Senior Citizens in all cities and most local areas to find out the help that is available. It is there and they are only too willing to help.

- It is essential that you keep a balance in your own life. Keep your own cortisol and Adrenaline levels down. Caring responsibilities are but one aspect of your life though it may feel overwhelming at this time.

    - Don't feel like your life has to stop. You are not serving anyone if you get run down and sick and can't offer support.
    - Don't get 'the guilt's' if you miss visiting or calling for a couple of days. You may feel guilty but you could also be in for the long haul and need to keep a balance. Again get others on board to help with the caring. Share it out as mentioned above.
    - Keep yourself healthy.
    - What do you use to reduce your stress? Walking, camping, pictures, reading a book, socialising..... Do it!
    - Re-read some of the ideas in this book for yourself.

IDEAS to Reduce stress & the brain's stressful chemicals

- Engagement and a sense of hope are the key. This book is about ideas that will assist your loved ones to remain engaged with the world and maintain this sense of hope.

- Having someone listen to them and their concerns is so important. Be aware that you may listen to these concerns, worries and stories every visit, or within the same conversation, but that is ok. Your willingness to listen is so beneficial to them.

- Listening and interaction is essential.

This book is about ideas that will help reduce the stress of worry and feelings of uselessness. Be it music, videos, family, photos, craft, oral history reminiscing, these ideas are meant to help them experience a sense of life and purpose **"Now"**.

Challenge

Here is a challenge:
- Allow yourself five minutes to list twenty things you personally like doing e.g: Having coffee with friends, going to the pictures, beach walks, afternoon sleeps..
- If you find it hard to list twenty that is ok but just be aware.
- Now write beside each item you have listed when you did them last.
- If there are some you have not done for a while make a time to go and do them. They will help to sustain you and keep you clear and focused.

Ambiance - Room Decor

A lot of time when people go from independent to dependent living, they have to downsize, particularly if they have to move house or residence. This could be into a retirement village, nursing home or care home. In some instances they go from a house with numerous rooms to a one room residence of their own.

It's important that this room is stimulating and multi-sensory, that means that you look at things you can do to make this space feel like home. Using familiar items that have meaning to your loved one can be an excellent way of enhancing their quality of life.

Top Tip

Fresh flowers activate the senses – visually, smell, touch, memory. Here is a great idea, organise four wage earners in your family or friendship circle who are prepared to have an automatic monthly deduction of $40 ($10 a week) each to assure that a fresh arrangement of flowers can be delivered weekly to your loved one

Ideas

- Photos of family, home, events etc.
- Wall decals, these are removable and depict a variety of scenery such as beach views through a window, life size bookshelf that can be put on a door, telephone boxes and you can get your own original design made up as well.
- Is there one or two pieces of familiar furniture which can be brought from home?
- Aromatherapy can be very powerful.
- Indoor plants.
- Grandchildren's art work from school is great to put up on the wall.
- Sporting club memorabilia.
- Music player; set it up to loop a favourite CD or program in their favourite radio stations.

Actions

Conversation Starters

The great gift of conversation lies less in displaying it ourselves than in drawing it out of others. He who leaves your company pleased with himself and his own cleverness is perfectly well pleased with you.

Jean de la Bruyere

Communication is vital for the human spirit. Unfortunately if we get isolated through distance, health or an inability to regularly interact and communicate with familiar people, our lives can become more insular and lonely. Many research papers have been done on the immense power of conversation and in particular being listened to and listening. It keeps the brain engaged and active and adds to our sense of worth.

There can be two challenges here dependent on our loved ones perceived mental ability. Sometimes the stories they tell are ones of their long ago past which we have heard many times before yet they are thinking they are telling us for the first time. This requires our loving patience as we listen as if it is the first time we have heard it. On the other hand we can feel the stories or our own daily lives are so ordinary that we will bore them or we get no response.

Sometimes, when we visit a loved one we are a little lost as to what to talk about. Here are some ideas which may help with the conversation.

Top Tip

When questioning or in conversation it is best to use open ended questioning techniques. This simply means questions that don't have a yes or no answer. An example – Did you finish primary school? vs What memories do you have of finishing primary school? The benefit of open ended questions is that they help to stimulate a number of memories and linkages within the brain's neurons. This will result in greater engagement and memory recall.

- Reminiscences about different times in their life or events – life's journey:

    - Place of birth and early life
    - School
    - Adventures of youth, dances, parties, holidays, sport
    - Working life
    - Courtship/marriage
    - New babies
    - Family holidays
    - Places where they have lived
    - Friends and interests
    - How times have changed
        - Transport
            Roads – cars, trains, buses, trams, planes, boats
        - Communication
            Letters, telegrams, telephone, mail, computers
        - Houses or places they have lived
        - Toilets over the years (there will be stories here for sure)
        - Magazines
        - Radio and TV
    - Events like storms, cyclones, fires
    - Important people in their lives
    - Any travel adventure and holidays they have been on
    - World events (war)

- Have you thought about reading to or with your loved one? Newspapers and magazines are a great way to explore what's happening and stimulate conversations.

- Do an oral history for the family in years to come - see specific chapter.

- Homemade memory/treasure bag – place items in a bag that have a special significance and take turns pulling one out and discussing why.

Examples of products to help

Age of Adventure

Generate meaningful, therapeutic conversations with your loved one. Age of Adventure is a photography-based set of cards depicting adventurous older people living their lives to the full. It can operate as a speech therapy tool, a conversation prompt or a challenge to stereotyping of older community members. Age of Adventure reinforces the idea that life doesn't have to stop when we age.

By Judi Fisher
Published by Innovative Resources in 2008

ColourCards: What Can You See?

This is an entertaining game which can be played by both individuals and groups. Each of the selection of pictures is viewed through a space in the book's pages, gradually revealing more and more of the image. This allows players to guess what they can see, encouraging communication. The set contains two viewing books, each with different panels, and 30 large-format (A4)cards.

Toss and Talk about Ball

This ball is an ideal way to add physical fitness and to your reminiscing sessions and is a good way to make them more fun. The original Toss 'n Talk-About Ball features 60 categories (for example, circus animals, flowers, tools). When the ball is caught, the player names three items that fit into a specific category that has been selected by the position of their thumb (60cm when inflated).

Life Times ColourCards: World War II

This set contains 48 photographic cards depicting life from 1939 to 1945, when daily experiences were defined by World War Two.

Subjects include:

- Army, Navy and Air Force
- School life
- Family life
- Evacuation
- Air raids and shelter
- Political figures
- Entertainment
- Home Guard
- Land Army
- Digging for Victory and many more...

 For more information on these products please go to
www.agedandengaged.com.au

Actions

Craft

Some people have a lifelong history of involvement with craft, others may be new to it. There are, however, many easy crafts that your loved one or those with limited dexterity, low vision and other physical or mental limitations can enjoy. Crafting provides creativity and a feeling of accomplishment.

Taking part in craft activities can be of benefit to everyone in more ways than simply creating something. It is an also a great way to promote social engagement, encourage tactile manipulation, design mind and promote a sense of achievement.

- For anyone living in a nursing homes or some form of assisted living, being involved with a craft can help them to make new friends and feel less isolated. Having a shared interest, such as crafting, brings people together and encourages a sense of belonging.

- Many people who live on their own find that crafting is an enjoyable pastime.

- Making crafts is a good way to keep the mind sharp and stimulated.

- The majority of crafts involve some degree of manual dexterity and using the hands helps to exercise fingers and hands.

- Working on crafts can help to reduce depression in some people.

Quality time

Is there a particular skill they have you've always wanted to learn / try?

Why not spend quality time together, doing a joint project?

If your loved one has a history of involvement with a particular craft, find out if there is a craft group that meets in their area. One of the members might even volunteer to drive them to and from a meeting. This is a great social outlet and also a good way for them to learn new skills and pass on their lifetime of learning.

Check out the various groups advertised on the internet at **www.meetup.com**.

Examples of Crafts

- Brush painting, finger-painting

- Scrapbooking with old photos or pictures out of magazines

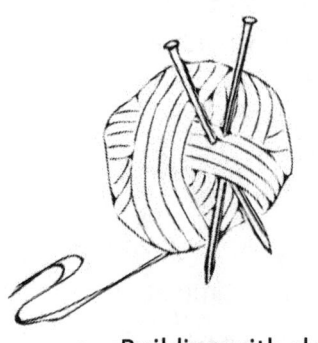

- Knitting and crocheting
  There a plenty of charities around where your loved one's knitting can be donated. Most places only need a 20cm square, which is relatively easy to do, and for the person who has always loved knitting and crocheting can be very enjoyable.
  (For example: www.knit-a-square.com)

- Building with clay

- Soap making

- Cooking classes

- Card making

- Flower arranging

- Model Building

- Woodwork

- Cooking, baking cakes

- Salt dough cooking

- Play dough

- Bead making

- Maquetry

- Leatherwork

Is there a local men's shed that your loved one can attend?

> "The modern Men's Shed is an updated version of the shed in the backyard that has long been a part of Australian culture. Men's Sheds are springing up all around Australia. If you looked inside one you might see a number of men restoring furniture, perhaps restoring bicycles for a local school, maybe making Mynah bird traps or fixing lawn mowers or making a kids cubby house for Camp Quality to raffle. You might also see a few young men working with the older men learning new skills and maybe also learning something about life from the men they work with. You will see tea-bags, coffee cups and a comfortable area where men can sit and talk. You will probably also see an area where men can learn to cook for themselves or they can learn how to contact their families by computer."

- Australian Men's Shed Association

Actions

DVD's

There are endless varieties of DVDs available today both in traditional format, or that can be viewed online or downloaded. They include movies, documentaries and there are also "DIYs/how to..." on just about any topic.

By using the questionnaire at the beginning of the book, we suggest you choose a couple of ideas which target your loved one's interests. For example: A DVD about "line dancing".

Top Tip

Have you investigated TV and DVD players with only ONE remote control? There are also devices that can be operated by you in your home many kilometers away. See the chapter on available technology.

Here are a few suggestions of a general nature.

- **Ambient DVDs:** These involve scenes of nature with either relaxing music or the sounds of nature. Ambient DVDs have been programmed so that the tracks repeat automatically to facilitate endless relaxation.

    Examples of titles available:
    - Tropical Reef and Oceans Aquarium
    - A Day at the Tropical Beach
    - Campfire by the Beach
    - Ocean Waves
    - The Living Ocean – An Underwater Journey
    - Tropical Gardens and Butterflies
    - Rainforest Creeks

- Virtual Walk DVDs: A range of DVDs called Fitness Journeys and Nature Walks. Sit your loved one in front of a TV, play the DVD, and they can go for a virtual walk. Speeds range from a walk to running or biking speed, with most of the tracks being a jog or fast walking pace. These virtual walk DVDs use the sounds of nature to further enhance the natural experience. These are fantastic for loved ones who have previously been a walker, jogger or runner but are unable physically to do so anymore.

  Examples of titles available:
  - Journey through the Forest
    (five different journeys to choose from)
  - Tropical Scenery
  - Forest Walk (virtual walk under the shady trees)
  - Through the Mountains (five different journeys to choose from)
  - Romantic Paris
  - Ancient Rome

- Relaxation DVDS: Scenes of nature with relaxing background music.

  Examples of titles available:
  - Coral Reef Dreaming
  - Dolphins at play
  - Relaxing with Nature
  - Waterfalls of the Daintree
  - Beautiful Blooms
  - Tasmania's Overland Track

- **Reminiscence DVDs:** DVD movies with slideshow presentations of still photographs with no captions or narration just background music to enable easy listening, viewing and an opportunity for reminiscence.

    Examples of titles available:
    - Awesome Aviation
    - A Day at the Show
    - A Day at the Zoo
    - Australia's Coast from the Air
    - Maritime Mix CD
    - Marvellous Machinery
    - Outback Adventure
    - Wonderful Wheels (old time cars)
    - A Flower Medley
    - Gone Fishing
    - In the Garden
    - Old time Music Machines
    - Moments in Lavender
    - Oranges and Lemons
    - The Vegetable Patch
    - Getting Around

Actions

Games

Playing board games and cards with your loved one is a great way to spend quality time in a non-demanding way whilst keeping them engaged.

Using the questionnaire again, find out what board and card games have they played and enjoyed in the past.

Dependent on their ability, additional examples could include peg boards and magnetic boards.

- Canasta, Bridge, Five Hundred
- Chess
- Rummikub
- Large pieced puzzles - make your own photo puzzles
- Bingo games
- Card games - memory games
- Activity aprons
- Large dice games
- Sorting buttons or beads
- Flash cards - make and print your own, with pictures or photos
- Chalk boards

- Magnetic boards – you can use a baking tray with different sorts of magnets
- Traditional board games (e.g. Monopoly)
- Shape and color sorting - you can buy or make your own using buttons etc
- Puzzles
- Large printed cards
- Hard holders
- Ring toss
- Handbag sorting – fill a handbag with all sorts of items that your loved one would enjoy going through and seeing what's in there.

- Snooker/pool

- Coin tossing

- **Tool boxes** - you can buy versions that your loved one can sort through.

- Cork boards with nails and hammer.

- Card games

- Cup stacking

- **Painting or sanding** - bird boxes?

- Bocce

- **Carpet bowles** - this is a great group activity.

- **Scrapbooking** - with old photo's or magazines.

- Baby dolls for your loved one to care for.

Examples of products available
Believe it or not, a lot of these games can be sourced through children's educational suppliers or shops.

Life Stories

This storytelling game is a great game to play with your loved one to help find out more about their past life. This game allows different generations of family and friends to talk and share opinions. The questions act as prompts to recall memories, reveal hopes and dreams.

Grandparent Talk Conversation Cards

This set of portable conversation questions is a good way to uncover family stories that haven't been shared in years. You choose a card, ask the question and watch your family history unfold. The game keeps family history alive with diverse topics that allow children, grandchildren and grandparents to discover more about each other.

The cards are attached to a carabineer clip for easy portability and each clip contains 100 cards.

Historic Early Aviation Playing Cards

Anyone interested in the history of flight will enjoy looking at these cards. Each of the 52 coloured pictures depicts a dirigible or other aircraft, up to the final card which represents the Wright Brothers. Original 1910 text is included on each card.

Shake Loose a Memory

Shake Loose a Memory is a game for people who are memory impaired. It is designed to unlock memories by reconstructing everyday life experiences. The game includes 192 memory-stimulating cards aimed at starting discussion and prompting memory. For example: "Keep this card if you have grown a garden. Remember planting vegetables?".

Shake Up the Relatives

This games helps people to recall close family members and their unique qualities. Questions include "Did your grandmother like to bake homemade bread or did she like to buy it from the store?" and "Did your father wear glasses or did he have good eyesight?" Relatives can be brought to mind and remembered through sharing stories.

Antique Motor Cars Playing Cards

Antique car enthusiasts will love these playing cards, featuring 54 turn-of-the-century motor cars, including some of the earliest cars manufactured around the world. The images and descriptions are taken from 1920s advertising insert cards.

Actions

Gardening

Gardening is a lifelong love for so many people and getting old does not mean that you can no longer use your green fingers.

Here are some ideas for people who are still active and those who may not be:

- Raised garden beds -Timber boxes or galvanised garden beds that raise the plants up to waist height enabling the gardener to move around without having to bend over or too far in. These can be bought at various large nurseries and hardware stores or you can make them yourself.

- Windowsill gardens

- Plant Trolly - If your loved one is bedbound, how about creating a garden on wheels? Create a plant trolley containing pot plants or small punnets of flowering plants that give out a lot of fragrance and which can also provide a tactile experience.

- Herbs, fruit and vegetables

- DVD on gardening

- Magazines on gardening with lots of colour

- Gardening calendars

- Picture books, books on trees, landscapes and gardens.

- Can you organize a weekly flower arrangement delivery ?

Quality time

Take a trip to the garden centre – most have cafes now so look around, have a drink etc. low cost and local.

Examples of products

Gardening Projects for Horticultural Therapy Programs

This book is full of ideas for horticultural therapists and activity professionals who work with elderly people. The book contains themed gardening activities for a wide range of abilities.
These activities open up avenues for socialisation, opportunities to relive memories and make new discoveries and make an ideal way to share a love of gardening.

Indoor Garden on wheels

Create a plant trolley containing pot plants or small punnets of flowering plants that give out a lot of fragrance and which can also provide a tactile experience.

Planter kits

This colourful planter, full of gorgeous succulents would make a great gift for anyone who loves gardening and plants. You can buy the planters and put whatever type of plants you require in them.

Gardening for Seniors:

Joyous Activities for Elderly Gardeners with Tips for Reduced Mobility

This book contains a wide range of information that will inspire your loved ones to continue, or start, gardening.

Garden spaces, tools and equipment can be modified or adapted to help reduce the physical stress associated with gardening. Suggestions include:

- Using vertical planting to make garden beds accessible for planting and harvesting – try using wall and trellis spaces

- Using retractable hanging baskets, wheelbarrows and containers on castors to make suitable movable and elevated garden beds

- Finding adaptive tools and equipment – these are available from some hardware shops

- Using foam, tape and plastic tubing to modify existing tools for a better grip

- Using lightweight tools that are easier to handle

- Providing areas of shade for working in summer months

- Having stable chairs and tables to use for comfortable gardening

- Making sure that there is a tap nearby or consider installing a drip feeder system for easy watering.

Actions

Gifts

For birthdays, mother and fathers' days, Christmas, anniversaries and weekly visits, we love to give and receive gifts but

"What will we get them?"

There are some great gifts available for your aged loved one. Again use the questionnaire at the beginning of this book to focus on their interests, then use some of the ideas in this book. Additionally, it sometimes only takes a bit of research and bit of thinking outside the square.

- **Anniversary DVD or Birthday DVD:** This is a unique gift for a senior or a couple celebrating a special anniversary. Original newsreel from news, world events, music, sports, entertainment. The DVD only mentions the year, so you can use for a range of occasions. It includes narration and music from that year. Any year you might be interested in from 1929 all the way through to 1981 is available. The anniversary and birthday DVDs are 30 minutes in length, black and white. The cover design may vary depending on the year. (www)

Quick Win

Jigsaw puzzles and photo puzzles can be made from their own photos (e.g. their family home).

- Photo books that you can make on the internet through major retail shops and local print shops. It is now so easy to get photos of particular events or periods of one's life bound into a book.

- You can also make your grandparents photo mugs, keyrings etc

- Handcrafted presents from great grandchildren are always a favourite. These could be photo frames, cards or scrap books containing family photos.

- Handmade soaps and powders
- Books
- Canes
- Pot plants
- Large print brain games
- Calendars
- Perfume
- Photo presents or frames
- Lap trays - for eating
- PJs and slippers
- Digital clocks
- Tap on led lamps
- eReader tablet pillow/aids
- www.Gifts with Bling

Actions

Internet

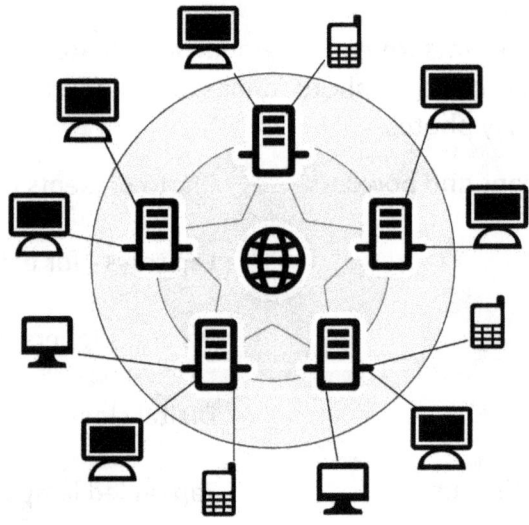

Now days the internet is part and parcel of everyday life, we use it daily. It makes life easier in so many different ways, from paying bills to viewing pictures and talking to the grandkids who may live on the other side of the country with ease.

To access the internet there are many different ways such as tablets, smart phones, laptops, pc's and smart tv's. Finding what will work the best for your loved one is the key here, we have listed some options in our technology chapter.

With the thousands of websites out there which can be fantastic resources for your loved one as well as the family, we have decided just to mention a few key ones.

Websites to help your loved one become more computer savvy......

Good50.com
Good50 is a Google search engine that has been adapted to be easier to read and more user-friendly to everyone who needs it, including senior citizens. Good50 is powered by Google and, therefore, produces the same high quality search results in a different format.

www.good50.com

gcflearnfree.org
GCFLearnFree is an online learning platform with courses in technology, literacy and maths. The site lists around 750 lessons that are available for basic and intermediate levels. The design of the site is generally suitable for the older person and helps them gain internet and computer skills. There are a number of technical courses, including how to use an ATM. Courses are interactive and supported with articles, videos, and animation.

www.gcflearnfree.org

skillfulsenior.com
Skillful Senior, an American site, which teaches basic computer navigation skills. The focus here is teaching the elderly how to access health information on the web. The site has interactive animated tutorials, which teach your aging relative how to use the mouse, the arrow keys on the keyboard and touch typing. Importantly, they also teach about ergonomics too, so that the elderly can use the computer without sitting badly and causing themselves pain. Each tutorial has a voice-over by a digital character to explain everything as you go along.

www.skillfulsenior.com

curious.com
Instructors on this site can upload videos on any subject, from salsa dancing to making cocktails, broken up into easy lessons. Unlike YouTube, teachers on Curious can charge, although most are free. The site generally feels friendly and constructive and there is an oversize playback window. The site's proprietors currently approve teachers and content to ensure that these online classes remain upmarket.

www.curious.com

Microsoft Guide For Aging Computer Users
This site provides helpful tips on how to make the computer experience more comfortable as you get older. It deals with screen resolution, text size, colour, speech recognition and shortcuts among other things. The easy-to-use format helps older people to customise and personalise their computer and get the most out of the experience. A simple click brings up a step-by-step instruction page.

www.microsoft.com/enable/aging/tips.aspx

Newsworthy Sites

upworthy.com
This site provides lots of uplifting and inspirational content that is very easy to navigate and to share via social media.

www.upworthy.com

www.news.com.au
The national news website for Australia. The site has a good cross-section of news and is free to peruse.

www.news.com.au

Social Media Sites

Facebook
Facebook is the world's most popular social networking website. It makes it easy for you to connect and share with your family and friends online and is very simple to join and use.

www.facebook.com

Twitter
Twitter is an online social network and real-time communication service launched in 2006 and used by millions of people and organisations to quickly share information. The word "Twitter" relates to the chattering sound made by birds, hence the bird used in the Twitter logo. Users can access the site via the web and mobile devices to exchange frequent bite-size updates of information called 'tweets', which are messages of up to 140 characters long that anyone can send or read.

www.twitter.com

Pinterest
Pinterest is like a virtual bulletin or cork board that allows users to find and curate images and videos. It's a very easy way to find things on the internet and is highly addictive.

www.pinterest.com

Instagram
Instagram is an online photo-sharing, video-sharing and social networking service that enables its users to take pictures and videos, apply digital filters to them, and share them on a variety of social networking services, such as Facebook, Twitter, Tumblr and Flickr.

www.instagram.com

Google plus
Google+ is a social networking and identity service owned and operated by Google Inc. It is the second-largest social networking site in the world.

www.google.com

Brain Health

Brain Bashers
Collection of brain teasers, puzzles, riddles, games and optical illusions updated regularly.

www.brainbashers.com

Brain Metrix
Brain training exercises to build memory, improve reflex, and "brain creativity".

www.brainmetrix.com

Sudoku Online
Designed to keep your mind active with "billions" of online Sudoku puzzles organised into different skill levels.

www.websudoku.com

Luminosity
Build your personalised brain training program, available online, tablet or mobile.

www.lumosity.com

CogniFit
An award-winning brain fitness software program created by CogniFit, that assists the senior population with the decline in cognitive abilities. It has dedicated software for driving skills designed to maintain and enhance these abilities in adult drivers.

CogniFit's personalised brain fitness programs are unique because they begin with a personal assessment that determines the state of your cognitive health and then create a training system that continuously charts your progress and adapts itself to your changing needs while you use it.

www.cognifit.com

Other

CaringBridge
An invaluable resource for families experiencing a major health challenge with a loved one, a stay in hospital for example. Caring Bridge allows you to create a website (at no charge) to keep everyone in the loop with updates on health status, test results, visiting hours, and other related news.

www.caringbridge.org

Love to Know: Seniors
This site offers perhaps more than you ever wanted to know about seniors, and even includes information for senior nudists! This is an American site but contains some useful information.

www.seniors.loveto know.com

Your Life Choices
An Australian website that covers health, wealth, travel and work for the over 50s and senior citizens.

www.yourlifechoices.com.au

Legals

There are some really important legal documents that need to be discussed and organised.

Approaching this can be tricky and ideally should be done by all of us when we are younger. The reality is that these discussions haven't occurred on many occasions and can certainly lead to challenges as we get older or if we get seriously ill.

Legal documents include Power of Attorney for both financial affairs and health directives.

Top Tip

These discussions can get more difficult as time passes but it is a discussion that needs to happen.

Our suggestion is that you do this NOW and also arrange your own affairs NOW, no matter what age you are. These are discussions that are best dealt with early.

A properly prepared 'Will' is also very important. This again, should be done when we are clear about our wishes. You can do these with DIY kits if you are confident, or under the guidance of legal practitioners. You don't want your wishes taken out of your hands and given to a State appointed Adult Guardian or Trustee if you were to become suddenly ill and deemed incapable of making decisions.

- Ask your loved one if they have made a Will.
- Have they appointed their Power of Attorney -Financial and Legal.
- Arrange an appointment with a Legal Professional for them to do this or get a DIY kit off the internet.
- Give them information to read about these documents. Give them a You Tube clip to watch.
- Ask them to tell someone where they are storing these documents and who this person is..
- What are their funeral wishes?

Actions

Manipulation & Tactile

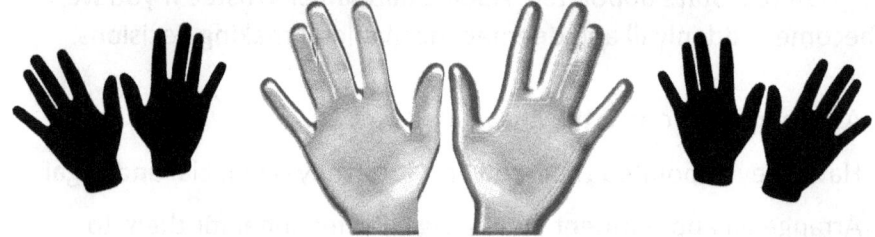

The ideas expressed here are for people in care and at home and will depend on ability. Tactile sensations are very important, which is why crafting is so good. Here are some other ideas we found.

- Fiddle boxes - Ranging from soft shapes, materials and toys to old fishing reels and boxes of plumbing pieces to put together. Female and male sorting and fiddle boxes can be made up as required.
- -Vary the texture and things your loved one can do with them.

- Cloth pets (small puppies and cats) to hold on lap and stroke.

- Activity aprons and table mats. Include various textures, zips, buttons. These fit on table tops and over chairs, so that people who are restricted to a chair can still enjoy tactile stimulation.

- Fiddle cushions

- Singing Teddies. These are teddy bears that sing various themed songs.

- Zen garden with sand and small rake. 30cmx 15cm is big enough.

- Play dough, clay, wax or plasticine

- Homemade memory/treasure bag – place items in a bag that have a special significance and take turns pulling one out and discussing why.

Examples of products

Actimat

Contains everyday items to stimulate memory, motor skills and cognitive function. Actimat has been created with the needs of those suffering from dementia and stroke in mind. It will also help anyone suffering from acquired brain injury to re-develop motor skills.

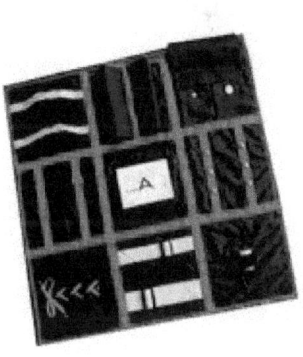

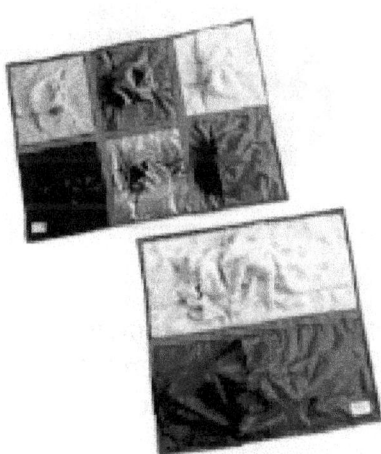

Feelymats

Feelymats have been designed to stimulate anyone suffering from dementia by means of touch. The mats come in two or six textures and can also aid rehabilitation after digital nerve damage.

Men's Activity Pillow

This activity pillow has been designed to help men suffering from dementia stay engaged. A denim mat with a variety of features, such as flannel pieces that button over patterned fabric and corduroy pieces that lace over a vinyl picture frame which can hold a favorite photo. The padded pillow can easily be securely to an over-chair tray.

Soothing Pat Mat

A calming, sensory stimulation aid, ideal for anyone suffering from the pain of arthritis. The Pat Mat can be filled with distilled warm water to ease stiff joints in the hands or cool water to help take the heat out of a summer's day.

Twiddle Sport

Twiddle™Muffs are designed to provide activity to aid brain stimulation and have a calming effect. Available in a range of designs, Twiddle Sport Muff comes in blue and green plaid and contains a squeezable ball in middle as well as other interchangeable features.
Each Twiddle™ Muff is equipped with detachable stimulating gadgets such as a sealed satin bag containing marbles, strand of textured ribbons, loop of colourful wooden beads, soft, smooth satin or faux suede pocket and a Velcro tab patch.

Actions

Music & Auditory

Across all cultures in the world, music is present

The power of music cannot be underestimated for any age or ability group. It cuts across cultural boundaries and is found in all traditions. It stimulates all the senses and evokes brain activity, memory, rhythm and makes you feel good. It can be pleasurable for individuals or as a group activity. Sing-along's are a great example of this.

Now days there are many different way to access music. First you need to know the sort of music they love:

Music CDs: Old time favourites can include:

- 40s era
- 50s era
- 60s era
- Big Band
- Vaudeville
- Classic
- Country of origin folk/native music
- Jazz
- Big Band
- Instrumental
- Country
- Folk
- Australiana
- Sing-a-long

Suggested singers / groups:

- Glenn Miller
- Vera Lynn
- The Andrews Sisters
- Nat King Cole
- Come Dancing in the 30s, 40s and 50s triple CD Collection
- Mantovani and Friends

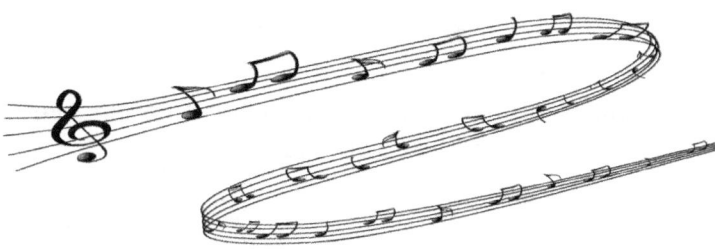

Digital Music

There are lots of different ways to access digital music in today's society, either for free or by paying per track or album. Digital music can be played through any device that is connected to the internet. If downloaded it is available offline whenever you want it.

Websites include:

Amazon

Amazon is one of the top stores for purchasing music, and it is also one of the very best for downloading free music. The massive online retailer currently lists over 50,000 songs for free download. Many of these are from rising artists competing to gain the attention of pop music fans. Amazon also does a great job of categorising the songs for easier browsing. This is an excellent way to discover new artists.

www.amazon.com

Free Music Archive

The Free Music Archive was launched in April 2009 by Jersey City radio station, WFMU, but personnel from other radio stations help to curate the music in the archive. The site is described as "a social music website built around a curated library of free, legal audio". The cost of the archive has being partially funded by the New York State Music Fund and people can donate directly to participating artists. This site includes clear guidelines on the permissible uses for the music, as determined by the artists themselves. Some tracks may be downloaded for listening only while others are cleared for use and distribution (e.g. background music for a video production).

www.freemusicarchive.org

Internet Archive's Audio Archive

The Audio Archive is a sub-project of the Internet Archive, which aims to collect and make available archived "snapshots" of internet content for researchers and the general public. As well as music, the Audio Archive includes audio books, news broadcasts and old time radio shows. The music collection numbers over 50,000 recordings all available for free download.

www.archive.org

Music-Streaming options in Australia

A music-streaming service is almost a radio station that you can program by genre, artist or mood. The music is played through a device which is connected to the internet – such as laptop, mobile, computer or tablet. You can then hook these devices up to a bluetooth speaker to be able to listen. Some music-streaming can be controlled remotely by a carer if your loved one is not able to work the device that the music is streaming to for themselves.

Most offer you the ability to stream unlimited music, but some also have provision for streaming via mobile, downloading for listening without an internet connection and streaming to other devices through the home. Some services have a wider selection of tracks than others, it would be best to have a quick search around the service or use a free trial to see whether there are enough songs that are appropriate. There is a cost involved with most music-streaming services and it can range from $5 a month to $12 a month. Some of them are free as long as you are happy to see/listen to advertising.

Here is a list of some of the music-streaming services offered in Australia as at February 2014:

Deezer
Deezer has a catalogue of over 25 million tracks to choose from. Originally a French service, Deezer is now available in Australia. Users have access to a range of promotions such as album streams before the official release date and gig tickets.

iTunes Radio
iTunes Radio is available through iTunes on Mac and PC, the Music app on iOS, and Apple TV.

iTunes Radio works in a similar way to other music-streaming services by offering a stream of songs based on artists and genres from your library. Where iTunes Radio differs from its competitors is its tight integration with the iTunes Store. So, if you like a song that's playing, you can click to buy the track instantly using your existing account.

Google Play Music All Access

All Access includes the features of the regular Google Music service, such as being able to upload 20,000 of your own tracks, as well as adding the benefits of streaming music from a library of 20 million tracks.

All Access also includes a radio service that lets you skip as many tracks as you like. Personalised radio stations can be created, or All Access will do the hard work for you, providing recommendations based on your current library, and other playlists you might enjoy. Songs can also be purchased on Google Play.

Songs can be pinned or cached offline for listening without an active internet connection.

Guvera

An Australian, ad-supported service where users can stream full tracks through the web interface or mobile apps for free.

Guvera's catalogue includes 10 million tracks, with popular new releases available as well as a decent range of independent artists. Users can search by artist or discover music through playlists. Music news and content is provided through a partnership with the Music Feeds website. Curation includes guest playlists and top tracks.

For the mobile apps, songs can automatically be downloaded for listening once a song has been played in part.

Sony Music Unlimited

Music Unlimited is Sony's integrated music-streaming service and was previously known as Qriosity. Music Unlimited works across a range of Sony devices, including the PS4, PSP, Sony internet-enabled TV, Walkman, Blu-ray player and home-theatre system and through the web interface. The comprehensive catalogue contains over 10 million tracks.

Pandora

Pandora offers a way to enjoy listening to music without choosing individual tracks and has become known as "internet radio". You enter the name of a favourite artist and Pandora will stream music of a similar sound and genre, providing an instant playlist without the need for you to put it together yourself.

This feature makes Pandora more like listening to the radio and differentiates it from the other services available. There are few ads and these tend to promote Pandora's own material. You can save artist stations as favourites and even block those you don't like.

Pandora is accessed via the web interface or the user-friendly iOS and Android apps. You need to have a free account to use the app, but this gives you access to any saved artist playlists. Due to licensing restrictions, you can only skip six songs per hour, per station, up to 12 skips per day.

Spotify

Spotify has a catalogue of over 20 million tracks.

The desktop interface is very similar to iTunes, featuring a playlist and shortcut list in the left column, with track selection and current tunes in the centre panel.

JB Hi-Fi Now

JB Hi-Fi's music-streaming service has an uncluttered web interface which makes it very user-friendly and is the only one on offer from an Australian retailer.

Once logged onto the service, JB Hi-Fi Now is simple to use. You can search using the standard search bar at the top of each page, by genre through the "Discover" window, by browsing mixes or by radio-like streaming. It also lets you look at profiles of other users and find songs that they like by filtering via age, gender and location. If you browse the catalogue by album, the service will highlight similar artists that you might enjoy. The apps have a similar clean layout to the web interface.

Examples of products

- **Music for Alzheimers/Dementia (5 Cds+DVD)**
  This six-disc set includes four hours of great musical classics, enhanced by Altus Oscillation, which have been chosen for Alzheimer's/dementia patients who are 70-years of age and older. It contains big band medleys, vocal standards collection, light classical favourites and instrumental standards.
  Another music CD— **Meditation for the Caregiver** —is also included.

  So, what makes this set special besides great songs and outstanding performances? Through a patent pending process called **Altus Oscillation**, various gentle stimulating wave impulses, already present in the brain, are harmoniously united with recognisable music, producing a listening experience much more therapeutic than music alone. There are **no invasive stimuli or pharmaceuticals** involved in Altus Oscillation and utilising the system is as simple as turning on a CD player. In national surveys, caregivers have said that their patient's mood and behaviour improved enough during the music sessions that they were able to find some **personal free time and relaxation**.

- **Steam Glorious Steam CD**
  Audio CD of the sound of Britain's great steam locomotives recorded by Peter Handford on location during the glorious days of steam.

- **Hear Memories CD and Booklet**
  This reminiscing resource CD includes sound scenes of yester-year ranging in length from 30 seconds to two minutes. The companion activity book for the CD includes reminiscing questions for each topic, as well as prop and music suggestions. It also Includes 14 sound scenes (trains, kitchen, farm, factory, city traffic, horse race, children's playground, water sounds, county fair, harbour sounds, pond, zoo, thunderstorm, and baseball game); plus 25 mystery sounds that can be used as a guessing game (typewriter, billiard balls, sawing wood, fog horn, sewing machine, telephone, rooster, crow, and 18 more).

Actions

Oral History

We all have stories to tell, stories we have lived from the inside out and so do our elderly loved ones. Often we forget this until it is too late and our loved one has either passed away or is in no fit state to be able to tell their story.

Oral history listens to these stories. Oral history is the systematic collection of living people's testimony about their own experiences. If we do not collect and preserve those memories, those stories, then one day will disappear forever.

With technology available these days it's very easy to record both audio and visuals. For example: webcams, video camera, smart phone camera or audio recording app, dictaphones.

Your loved ones' stories and the stories of the people around them are unique, valuable treasures for your family. You and your family members can preserve unwritten family history using oral history techniques.

When questioning or in conversation it is best to use open ended questioning techniques. This simply means questions that don't have a yes or no answer. An example – "Did you finish primary school?" compared to "What memories do you have of finishing primary school?" The benefit of open ended questions is that they help to stimulate a number of memories and linkages within the brain's neurons. This will result in greater engagement and memory recall.

- Use an external microphone for better sound quality. This also applies to video.

- Compile a list of topics or questions – keep it simple as you can always come back.

- Start each recording with a statement of who, what, when, and where you are interviewing.

- Listen actively and intently.

- Speak one at a time.

- Allow silence. Give your loved one time to think. Silence will work for you.

- Ask one question at a time.

- Follow up your current question thoroughly before moving to the next.

- Start with a few easy questions.

- Ask more probing questions later in the interview.

- Limit interviews to about one to two hours in length or even shorter, depending on the fatigue levels of you and your loved one.

- Save your recording for the future.

Possible topics about different times in their life or events:

- Place of birth and early life
- School
- Adventures of youth, dances, parties, holidays, sport
- Working life
- Courtship/marriage
- New babies
- Family holidays
- Places where they have lived
- Friends and interests
- How times have changed
    - Transport
    - Communication
    – letters, telegrams, telephone, mail, computers
    - Houses or places they have lived
    - Toilets over the years (there will be stories here for sure)
    - Magazines
    - Radio and TV
- Events like storms, cyclones
- Important people in their lives
- Any travel adventure and holidays they have been on
- World events (war)

Actions

"An oral history interview is something quite out of the ordinary because you are creating a historical document in those moments that you're sitting together. No paper documents exist to create the world through these narrative."

- Dr Marthe Norkunas

Personal Care

Personal Care consists of those tasks a person would normally be able to do as part of their normal daily functioning, but are unable due to a particular health issue, illness, disability or frailty. Some of these everyday tasks can have quite a significant meaning such as the hairdressing appointment that your loved one may have had every 2 weeks for the last 20 years or the monthly pedicure that signified that this was 'their own time' away from the stresses of family or general life.

Recommended

What about organising someone to drop around and have a chat if the family are too busy to do it regularly??

Here are some ideas that could help

There are private and charitable organisations that will come into the home and help with personal care tasks which could include:

- Showering or bathing
- Dressing including assistance with compression stockings
- Grooming
- Getting in and out of bed
- Toileting or continence management
- Personal hygiene
- Mobility within the house
- Hoist and lifting machine assistance
- Prompting to take medication
- Meal preparation
- Assistance with going to the shops, or appointments
- Payment of accounts
- Assistance to attend day programs or socialisation activities

If your loved one is in an aged care home most of the personal care aspects of their lives will be facilitated however there are other additional mobile options that you as family can organise. These services can be great for someone who is living at home as well.

- Massage therapist
- Acupuncturists / homeopath / naturopath
- Beautician
- Pedicure or manicure
- Personal trainer - to help with some gentle movements or exercise tailored to your loved one situation.
- Hairdresser
- Meals on wheels

Actions

Photo's

If you are lucky enough to have access to your loved one's photo collection this can be a treasure chest for ideas.

There a number of things that can be done here, especially if you have a lot of photos that are hard to keep stored, sorted and manipulated.

Photos: Can be scanned and made into a photo book around themes. These themes could include:

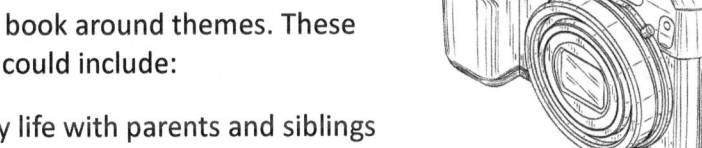

- Early life with parents and siblings

- Youth and pre-marriage times

- Marriage

- Family

- Books could centre around each of their children or grandchildren

- Holidays and adventure

- Places they have lived

- Pets

- Friends over the years

- Current photos are a great way to keep your loved one socially engaged even if they can't be there physically.

Jigsaw puzzles

Have you thought of getting familiar photos from any of the above and getting them made into a jigsaw puzzle. This can be done with various numbers of pieces to suit complexity. They can be made of cardboard, foam and wood.

- Most photo printing shops/online stores have the ability to make jigsaws out of your photos such as:
    - Printerstudio.com
    - Snapfish.com.au
    - Bepuzzled.com.au

- Create jigsaw puzzles of things that they love and have an interest in (e.g. vintage cars)

- These Photographic jigsaws can also be put on any electronic device such as an android tablet, iPad/iPhone/iPod or any touch screen computer with a finger dragging facility to move pieces around.

- IPHONE APPS
    - YourPuzzel
    - Amazing Puzzel Games HD
    - Bepuzzled.com.au

Photo Frames

Never underestimate the importance of the humble photo frame as a constant reminder of friends and family. Today you can choose from traditional frames or you can invest in electronic versions:

- Electronic photo frames: Upload photos onto an electronic photo frame and they will then slideshow continuously through all the images. These can be updated frequently to keep it interesting for your loved one.

- Use photos for a PowerPoint display and get your loved one to do the commentary. Most modern TV's will have a USB drive which can be used to view the images through the TV.

- Get crafty and make some frames - together or as presents.

- Decorate your loved ones room with plenty of images in a variety of forms.

Actions

Physical Activities

Regular physical activity is important to the physical and mental health of almost everyone, including your loved ones. Being physically active can help them continue to do the things that they enjoy and stay independent as they age. Regular physical activity over long periods of time can produce long-term health benefits. This is particularly applicable to the brain and keeping mentally fit ties in very neatly with physical fitness.

Often local council offices or libraries have a list of the interest groups formed in your area as well as the volunteer groups who specialize in helping people who need a bit more assistance. See if some ideas can be found here.

Recommended

Local Exercise Groups, Most gyms, PCYCs and Local Community Centres run regular exercise programs targeted at seniors. Volunteers are often available to help with transport and these are great places to improve physical fitness and also improve social interaction.

Some ways your loved one can keep physically active:

Chair Yoga

Modified yoga poses, that can be done while seated in a chair. These modifications make yoga accessible to people who cannot stand or lack the mobility to move easily from standing to seated to standing positions. In addition to a good stretch, chair yoga participants can also enjoy other health benefits of yoga, including improved muscle tone, better breathing habits, reduction of stress, better sleep, and a sense of well-being.

Exergaming

Using interactive video games to promote exercise. There are a number of different systems that you can exergame with including Xbox 360 Kinect, Wii Fit Plus and PlayStation Move.

There are hundreds of games that are suitable for your loved one such as bowling or fishing. The sensor technology is able to detect illness in seniors based on their physical positions while playing and can improve balance and hand-eye coordination as well as promoting laughter.

Game Activities can include:
- Sports
- Fitness
- Dance/Music
- Action Adventure
- Family

Tai Chi

This is a great form of gentle exercise with zero impact. It doesn't put too much strain on aging bones and joints. You can do Tai Chi from a seated position as well, which is great for your loved one who may be in a wheelchair or bedbound. You can find instruction videos on YouTube, DVDs or attend a class.

Walking

If you are visiting a housebound loved one, get them in a wheelchair and take them for a walk or taxi ride to the local shopping centre or around the block. Stimulate their interest and they will love it.

Actions

Reading

For many people in the aging demographic, book reading has been a lifelong passion. Even though their eyesight and concentration might not be as good as it once was, there are still lots of options available to allow them to continue reading.

Local libraries

Libraries have books with large type, audio books and access to local people who will read to others, there are also magazines, DVDs and games which you can take out on loan. Some councils have mobile libraries and it is worth finding out if they operate in your area. There are also groups who deliver these to local residents as a volunteer service. Contact the local library.

Once you join, your local library will give you access to a wide range of eBooks and eAudiobooks, music and videos, all available online anywhere, anytime. Most libraries allow you to use your library card number and PIN to borrow and download eBooks, eAudiobooks, music and videos for your compatible tablet, eReader, mobile phone, mp3 player or computer.

Quality time

Reading with grandchildren can be very powerful, this could also be done over distance using skype or facetime or webcam link.

eBooks

eBooks can be downloaded from the internet to be used on any computer, tablet, eReader, mobile phone or computer. Some you have to pay for but they are cheaper compared to hard copy books and there are thousands of free eBooks available. A great plus about eBooks is that you can easily change the settings on whatever device you are reading from, to increase the size of the text if your loved one has difficulty seeing. Most also have an audio read attached.

- iBooks app – iPads/iPhones
- Kindle Reader – downloads from Amazon.com website
- Booktopia.com.au
- Amazon.com.au
- kobobooks.com/Australia
- aureaderstore.sony.com/free_ebooks
- gutenberg.net.au/ – free eBooks from Australian writers

Audio Books

Audio books are fantastic for your loved one who can no longer read for long periods or for those who would just like the ease of being able to listen to a great book.

- soundbooks.com.au – audio books available on cd and tape
- audiobooksdirect.com.au – audio books available on mp3 cds
- shop.abc.net.au/t/formats/cd/audiobooks – ABC online shop
- Audiobooks from Audible – app for apple devices which allows you to download over 100,000 audio books from amazon.com
- iTunes store – download and listen to audiobooks

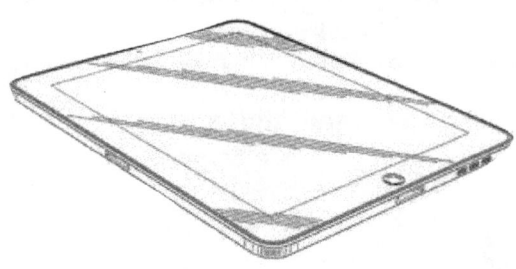

- Newspapers and magazines— can you read with them or to them? Discuss what's happening in the world. There are online versions for just about every publication these days.

- Magazines – these can be great visual stimulation, even for people who find it hard to read. Pictures can trigger all sorts of memories which in turn can lead to great conversations. Magazines are not just for women, don't forget the men – sporting, hobby, animal, motoring or technical.

- Subscriptions – magazines, newspapers, journals, blogs can all be set up for delivery in either hard copy or online.

Actions

Religious Beliefs

For many people, especially the aged, Religion has been an important part of their lives, be it public or private. This needs to be respected regardless of your own feelings. If your love one has a strong belief system this may very well be a tremendous support to them as they age.

Most churches have well established volunteer parishioners who are on roster as visitors and drivers to support the aged in their area. You don't have to have been a regular church goer to be part of their network. It is very often like Meals on Wheels where volunteers really enjoy visiting seniors, talking to them and providing transport to various social outings as well Religious services if that is what they want.

- Establish your loved ones feelings about Religion and its importance in their lives.
- Do/did they attend services regularly? Recent years or in the past?

- Would they like to talk to a Religious minister or pastoral worker? This is an important question to ask, especially if someone has been away from regular church attendance in recent times. They may really appreciate reconnecting with their faith even if you don't think they would.
- It is very easy to contact the local religious community and talk to them about your family member and see if they have a group who might visit them or offer support.

A discussion on religion, even if it is awkward, may be a discussion your loved one has been longing to have. You could ask directly or may slip it into a conversation when talking about their earlier lives.

Ideas

To support religious beliefs for those who are strongly religious:

- Online services
- DVDs or downloading of religious music
- Prayer or bible study books
- Religious icons of their particular faith:

    - Christian- Bibles. Prayer books, music, scripture readings. E.g. if they are Catholic possibly Holy Water, Rosary beads, statues, pictures
    - Islam
    - Buddhist
    - Other

Actions

Sport

For many people sport has been a lifetime passion and one of the best ways to engage and keep your loved one interested in life, is through sport. The preference is for them to maintain this participation, if at all possible. If they can't still play perhaps arrangements can be made for them to go to watch? Can you enquire if the local club would ask their members if anyone is able to drive them there to watch and socialize, if you can't. Can you get them looking through magazines or watch sport in the Sports channels or on DVDs. Read through this chapter on sports ideas to help stimulate your own thinking.

What sport was your loved one interested previously? Did they ever play sport in the past?

- Bowls
- Tennis
- Football
- NRL
- Rugby
- AFL
- Dancing

- Golf
- Horse racing
- Netball
- Surfing
- Sailing
- Swimming
- Cricket etc etc ....

Quick Win

Can they engage through a grandchild's sport?

Exergaming
Using interactive video games to promote exercise. There are a number of different systems that you can exergame with including Xbox 360 Kinect, Wii Fit Plus and PlayStation Move. There is a huge range of sport based games on several different kind of systems that are now available to purchase. Nearly every interest and sport is covered. They can become the virtual sport for those not able to actually participate.

DVDs
Can you get some DVDs for them to watch around their interest? (e.g football finals or horse races)

YouTube
YouTube have great videos on every sport imaginable – including memorable moments.

TV
Can you set up a sports channel for them? Again it must be easy to use or able to be operated remotely.

Spectating
Can your loved one go and watch live sport? Be that the grandkids or to a game of bowls?

Technology

Gerontechnology - or Technology for the older person

All of us are increasingly reliant on technology to assist our day to day living. There are now a wide range of technological solutions to help assist your loved one with their care needs.

> *"Gerontechnology can be defined as matching technology to health, housing, mobility, communication, and leisure and work of older people."*

Safety Technology

Safety technologies include technologies for emergency call and Personal Emergency Response Systems (PERS), fall detection and prevention, environmental monitoring (temperature, carbon monoxide, flood, smoke and fire alarms), access control, wander management, unattended stove shut-off systems and the like.

Safety technologies provide an enhanced sense of security, prolonged independence, improved quality of life and have the potential for improved health outcomes for your loved one.

Health & Wellness Technology

Health and wellness technologies include health promotion technologies, behavioural and health status monitoring systems, telehealth and telemedicine systems, as well as medication management technologies, which focus on the physical health and wellness of your loved one.

In addition, reminder systems and cognitive stimulation technologies, which focus on the mental health and wellness of your loved one, are also classified under this category. Some of the computer-based cognitive stimulation technologies have an entertainment value and some provide physical stimulation as well as sensory and cognitive stimulation.

- Cognitive Aids
- Electronic Health Records
- Health Promotion
- Monitoring
- Smart Home
- Telemedicine
- Wander Management

Social Connectedness Technology

Social connectedness technologies include phones (amplified, large-button, and memory phones), easy to use cell phones, which may offer, in addition to basic communication functionality, different communication modalities such as video reminders, multimedia messaging to keep loved ones connected with grandchildren.

Senior-friendly social networking websites, easy to use email systems, e-mail-to-paper communications systems, easy to use video phones and video conferencing systems also fall into this category.

These technologies provide increased social connectedness, improved quality of life and potential for improved health outcome for both loved ones and caregivers.

Examples of some of the technology available

Monitoring Technology
Just Checking

Just Checking monitors the movement of a person in their home and generates a chart of activity, online. The system helps people with dementia or poor memory to live independently in their own home. Just Checking is simple to install. There are no video cameras. The system uses wireless movement sensors and the mobile phone network. You don't need broadband, just a single power socket. This is an Australian based company.

www.justchecking.com.au

Communication

Jeenee Mobile – The telco for people who are older

This company believes technology should make your life easier. So they've taken the complexity out of using mobile phones and tablets and added in the things that people who are older need.

Like BIG easy to use icons to help make smartphones and tablets simple to use, 24/7 emergency BIG HELP giving you peace of mind and independence. We think that this provides exceptional service and good value for money, from a friendly Australian based company.

www.jenee.org.au

Computers / Laptops

There are many benefits of computer usage for your loved one and now days the type and price of computers whether they be laptop, desktop and /or touch screen are varied. Some benefits depending on your loved one's personal circumstances can include:

- Keeping in touch with family members. Webcams, instant messaging, and email simplifies the process of staying in touch with family members. The best part is that many of these tools are free.

- Improving motor skills and mental agility. Computer usage helps you stay sharp and mentally alert.

- Shopping On-line. Purchase items for yourself or others without having to leave the comfort of your home if desired.

- Paying household bills online and manage finances. No need to worry about missing payment dates or getting those pesky bill reminders in the mailbox.

- Using word processor with spell checker. A great option especially if physical limitations makes handwriting difficult.

- Interacting with your grandchildren on computer games you both enjoy. Having common interests with the younger generation is often a challenge. Becoming computer savvy with the latest games will make you super "cool" with the little ones.

- Researching health information and any other topics of interest. Internet tools such as Google and Yahoo, have the potential to make everyone an expert on virtually any topic.

- Reading the news or watching internet television. Stay in touch with current events or just relax while watching your favorite show with a click of the mouse.

The other thing worth remembering is that you can always get remote access to your loved one's computer from your own. It's a case of both computers being connected to the internet and then you can login from your own to your loved one's no matter where you are located, be it the next suburb or overseas. There is plenty of software available online to download and activate and most of them are free e.g. www.logmein.com or www.teamview.com

Tablets

There are many and varied tablets around that you can purchase for your loved ones, the main types are either Android or Apple.

Touchscreen technology makes it very simple for the older person to be able to operate.

Don't forget the accessories you can also get such as; holders either fixed to a table or with bigger hands for easy maneuvering, headphones, microphones, protective covers that keep off dust and liquids.

APPS

'App' is short for 'application' — another name for a computer program. Normally, when people talk about apps they are almost always referring to programs that run on mobile devices, such as smartphones, tablets or laptops.

Settings and Management

However, using and managing apps effectively can be difficult for many older people. Parental controls that exist to restrict children's activities also work well for senior users and enable you to help them to manage their computers, devices and apps. A Controlled User Account can restrict the number of options your loved one has access to, which not only helps avoid confusion, but stops them from launching programs accidentally. A Controlled User Account also gives you the option of setting up a remote login so that you can manage your loved ones online activities.

In order to simplify things, you should make sure that your loved ones have their apps and programs set to update automatically. In this way, they will always have the most up-to-date and secure versions of the programs they use.

Devices such as iPhones and iPads have several settings built in that can enhance usability. Look under settings/general/accessibility; VoiceOver, Zoom, Speak Selection, Dictation, Large Text and even Braille Displays for iOS to find what might help your loved one. These can help seniors with impaired vision and hearing to get the most out of their iOS devices. Android has similar settings, including TalkBack and Explore by Touch.

Some examples of apps:

ABC IVIEW
The stunning quality of iPad videos is showcased by this app, which lets viewers watch recent ABC shows at no charge. The iPad speaker produces decent sound or you can connect earphones for excellent audio quality.

Netflix
Most people use Netflix to order movies and other videos on DVD. This iPad app makes it easy to get many movies and TV shows streamed directly to the iPad for immediate viewing. Although the app itself is free, you need a paid Netflix account to download videos

iBooks
This is Apple's eBook app. Look for free books to download from Apple's iTunes store. Use the iBooks' controls to change type size and lighting and see if online reading is suitable for your loved one. Apple does not have as broad an eBook selection as Amazon, but you can download a free Kindle reader app that connects to Amazon and lets you read Kindle purchases.

Google Earth
Being able to see just about every location in the world is awesome. With the GPS capabilities of the iPad, you can always know where you are and how to get where you want to go. Use this app in conjunction with the Maps feature that is already loaded on the iPad.

Facebook Mobile

This app makes it much easier to communicate with others, but can also be used to play games. Many older people who play games via Facebook report that they feel less lonely and more content.

A Story Before Bed

Grandparents can read and record a story from the app's database and then the story is beamed to their grandchildren via webcam. During the progress of the story, an image of the reader appears in the corner of the screen, bringing everyone together. This app not only helps to combat elderly loneliness, but keeps grandparents in regular touch with their grandchildren.

Dragon Dictation, FREE

This app lets your loved one dictate text and then send it as an email message. They can also dictate reminders to themselves and post on Facebook and Twitter.

YouTube

An enormous collection of short videos which can be easily searched for and played. Everything from film clips to old news reels to pieces of music can be found on YouTube.

Skype

Skype is a fantastic way for older people to keep in touch with family and friends. All your loved one needs to do is push a button and call. As it has video and you can actually see the other person, it's almost like having a face-to-face conversation.

Real Racing 2 HD

This is an exciting driving game which is very easy to use and only requires the holder to tilt the iPad to steer and tap it to brake.

123D Sculpt, free

Your loved one can mould virtual clay with this extraordinary creative app.

iFish Pond

This app is great for anyone who enjoyed fishing in their earlier years but at the same time is a good all-round sensory experience for any individual. With the volume turned on, realistic water sounds are created every time the screen is touched. You can also use a virtual fishing rod to 'go fishing' by touching the screen. If you get a bite, drag your finger across the screen in a circular motion to 'reel in' your catch. This app has proved to be popular with care home residents because of its realistic appearance. As it's also very easy to use, it is ideal for individuals with advanced dementia.

Most of the above apps are also available on android devices and there are literally thousands of apps that may be suitable for your loved one – depending on what age and stage they are at.

Actions

Travel

Has your loved one travelled during their life?

- Can you make up a photo book of the various places they have travelled so they can look through and remember?

- Get some books on these places.

- Get some travel and discovery DVD of the places they have been.

- World map?

- Artefacts and memorabilia for them to see and touch.

Get them to be the travel guide to the PowerPoint collection you put together from their own travel photos.

Quality time

To aid your own research ask them where they have been. Get them to tell you about the trip and their adventures.

Countries travelled

- Australia and Oceania
- Africa
- Asia
- Europe
- Americas

TV Shows & Movies

Movies and television have played a big role in the lives of this demographic. Their lives began with silent movies, then the local cinema on a Saturday night, black and white television then colour. The world came into their lounge rooms and often became a great companion. Everyone had favourite shows and movies. What was theirs?

Television Programs

Game Shows

- Wheel of Fortune
- Family Feud
- Match Game
- The Price is Right

Comedy

- Dad's Army
- The Bob Hope Show
- Fawlty Towers
- Black Adder
- Yes Prime Minister
- Minister
- Open All Hours
- The Good Life
- Keeping up Appearances
- Are you being Served
- Some Mothers Do 'Ave 'Em

Dramas / Soap Operas
- Dr Who
- Carson's Law
- Class of 74
- Cop Shop
- A Country Practice
- Prisoner
- The Restless Years
- Home and Away
- Neighbours
- The Flying Doctors
- Sons and Daughters

Documentaries
- Travel
- Home and garden
- Grand design
- Animals
- Wilderness
- Food
- Family
- Cooking
- Craft
- Machinery
- Fishing

Movies
- Vintage
- 40s
- 50s
- 60s
- 70s

What was their interest? Look on the internet for some titles and classics. There might even be a local movie group who could help out here. These movies can be purchased, hired or downloaded. Just remember the operating machine needs to be simple to use (one switch or remote only).

Radio

Do they have some favourite radio shows that you could source for them? You can download onto MP3 or CD all the old time radio catalogue very easily. The programs can include adventure, comedy, detective, historical, serials, soap operas, quiz etc..

Actions

Conclusion

In conclusion we would again like to acknowledge that this time of transiting from independent to dependent living is a stressful time for both your loved ones and yourselves. It is important however that you see it as part of the journey. All you can do is to do your best. If this book has offered you some ideas to help keep your loved ones engaged with life we are very happy.

We have a website where we courage people to gain support from others and share their ideas on what has worked for them agedandengaged.com. We aso offer a consulting service for "time poor" family and friends, where we will help you source some of the ideas in this book based on the earlier questionnaire making sure all suggestions are specifically targeted.

www.ingramcontent.com/pod-product-compliance
Lightning Source LLC
Chambersburg PA
CBHW072010090426

42734CB00033B/2413